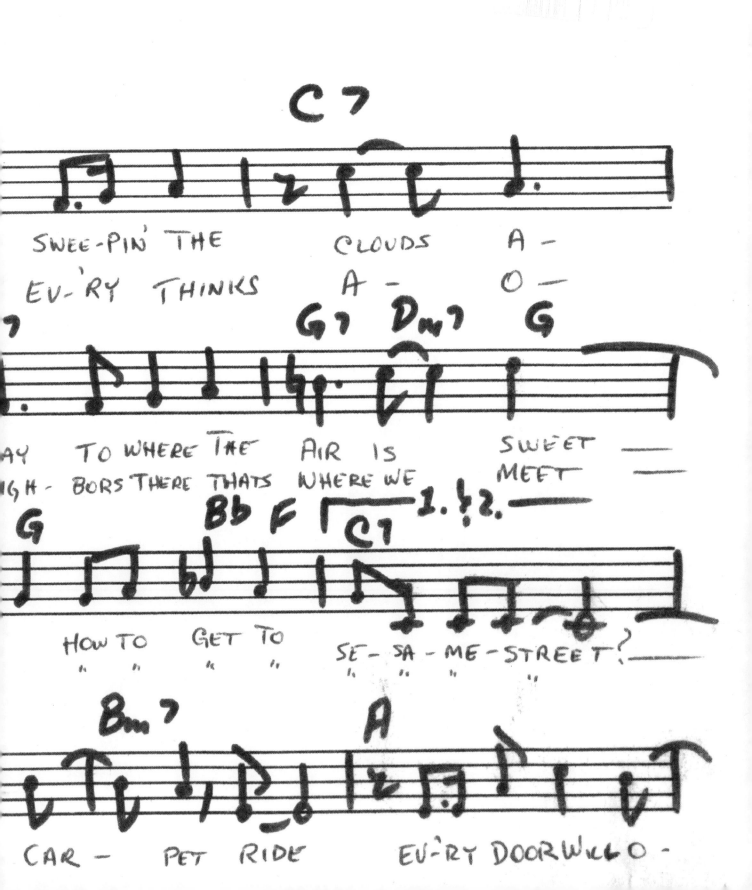

**C7**

SWEE-PIN' THE   CLOUDS   A -
EV-'RY THINKS   A -   O -

**G7**   **Dm7**   **G**

AY   TO WHERE THE   AIR IS   SWEET ___
IGH- BORS THERE THATS WHERE WE   MEET ___

**G**    **Bb F**   **C7**   **1. 2.**

HOW TO   GET TO   SE- SA - ME-STREET? ___
"   "   "   "   "   "   "

**Bm7**      **A**

CAR - PET RIDE   EV-'RY DOOR WILL O -

You've never seen
a street like
*Sesame Street.*
Everything happens
here. You're gonna
love it!

—Gordon's first lines on the first show

# SESAME

## UNPAVED

scripts, stories, secrets, and songs

written by David Borgenicht

CTW

HYPERION
New York

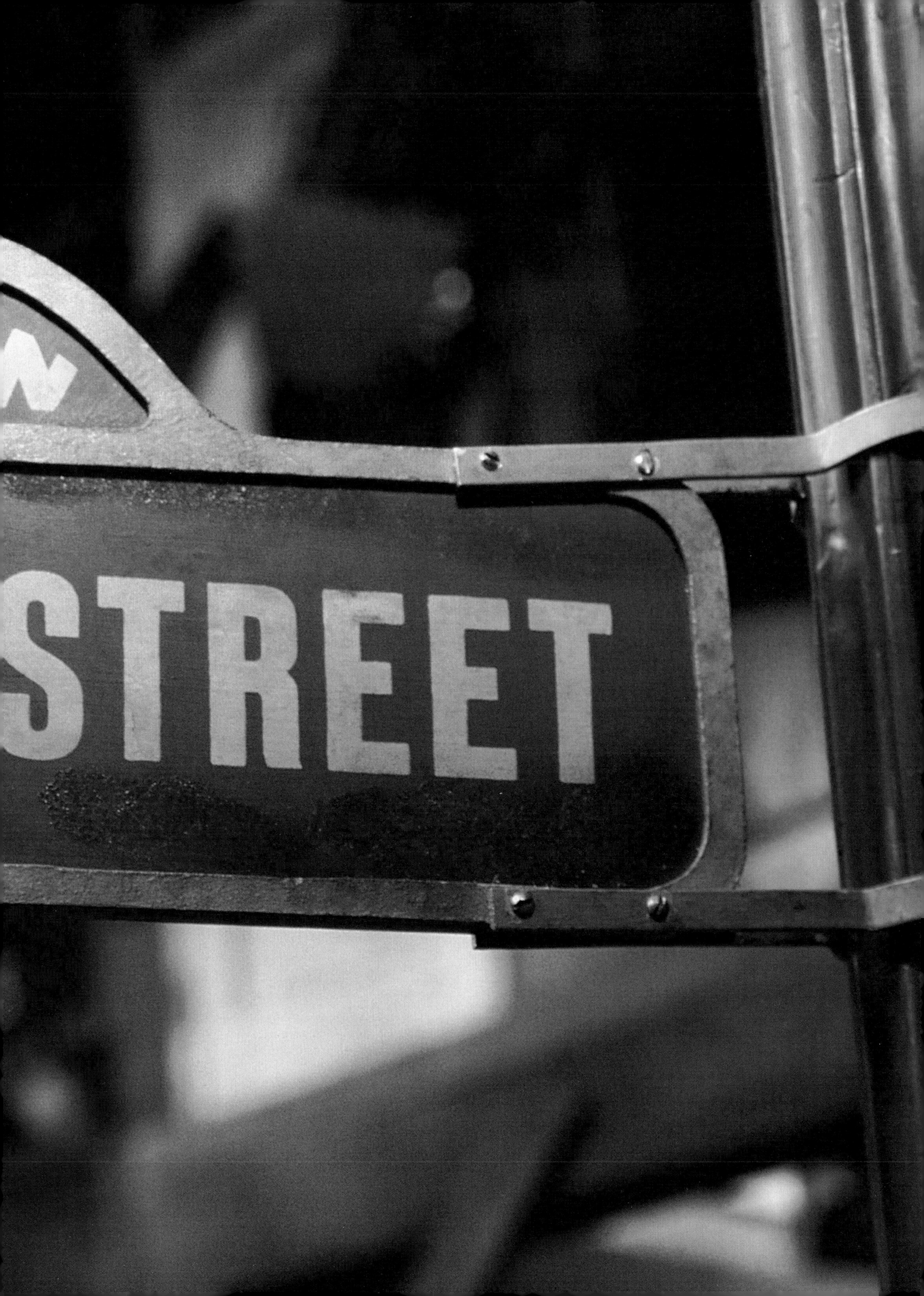
STREET

**To my family—MaNah MaNah**

A portion of the money you pay for this book goes to Children's Television Workshop.
It is put right back into *Sesame Street* and other CTW educational projects.
Thanks for helping!

One Lincoln Plaza, New York, NY 10023
www.ctw.org

Library of Congress Cataloging-in-Publication-Data
Borgenicht, David.
    Sesame Street: Unpaved: scripts, stories, secrets, and songs / by David Borgenicht. — 1st ed.
       p.   cm.
    ISBN 0-7868-6460-5
    1. Sesame Street (Television program)      I. Title.
    PN1992.77.S43B67   1998                                    98–6391
    791.45'72—dc21                                             CIP

Design and illustrations by Tanya Ross-Hughes, David Hughes/HOTFOOT Studio
Cover concept/illustration by HOTFOOT Studio

We wish to acknowledge the following photographers for their contributions to this book: John E. Barrett,
Charles Baum, Richard Hutchings, Eric Lebowitz, Don Perdue, Gary Randall/FPG International LLC,
Chrystie Sherman, Anita & Steve Shevett, Richard Termine, and Shonna Valeska

Cover photograph of Big Bird by John E. Barrett, cover background photograph by David Hughes
Cover photo art directors: Laurent Linn, David Hughes
Cover photo stylist: Danielle Obinger
Bert photo pg. 168 by © Shonna Valeska 1993

Special thanks from Hotfoot Studio to Lynne Yeamans, Kelly Holohan, Kristen Schilo, Joshua Lunsk for design assistance, and
Tanya Turner for photo permissions. Fonts used in design of this book: Ad Lib, Attic Antique, American Typewriter, Basketcase,
Coffeehouse, Fink Heavy, Kaixo, Klunder Script, Monterey, Spumoni, Superior, Treehouse, Univers, Vag Rounded, Will Robinson, Woodcut

Every effort has been made to determine copyright owners of photographs. In the case of any omissions,
the Publisher will be pleased to make suitable acknowledgments in future editions.

FIRST EDITION
10 9 8 7 6 5 4 3 2 1

# Acknowledgments

I know it's a cliché to say that this book could not have happened without the help of others, but *this book really could not have happened without the help of others.*

Huge thanks go to many people, but in particular: Joan Ganz Cooney for her vision and the drive that made the show happen and for teaching us all; all of the people who told us their wonderful stories and helped us gather information for the book, including Norman Stiles, Chris Cerf, Danny Epstein, Jeff Moss, Nina Link, Pam Green, Roscoe Orman, Loretta Long, Sonia Manzano, Bob McGrath, Emilio Delgado, Frank Oz, Jerry Nelson, Kevin Clash, Caroll Spinney, Debra Spinney, Martin Robinson, Fran Brill, Cheryl Henson, Jane Henson, Dulcie Singer, Gerry Lesser, Michael Loman, Arlene Sherman, Ed Christie, Lou Berger, and all the *Sesame Street* writers; All the people who are too many to count or name who helped us to dig through CTW's archives and allowed us to pester them again and again for scripts, clips, and info: Heather Dick, Kristen Presutti, Danette Desena, Lien Fu, Rodeena Stephens, Thelma Moses, Phil Bangle, Catherine Meiseles, Ian Luce, Barbara Stewart, David Chan, Lorraine Lipson-Velazquez, Julio Estien, Joseph Frilando, Rob Schuman, Rich Siegmeister, Sharon Lyew, Danielle Obinger, Karen Falk, Deborah November, and anyone else we've forgotten but meant to thank (you know who you are and you're probably not happy).

Extra-special thanks (and a publishing Emmy) go to: Stephanie Masarsky and Jenny Miglis, who deserve coauthor credit for doing an immense amount of research sifting through scores of scripts, tapes, photos, and helping to interview key players, and always knowing what to get for lunch; Tiffany Braby for keeping us organized, sane, and together; Laurent Linn for his keen artistic sense and input, and for his drink suggestion during dinner with Big Bird (whiskey sours); Betsy Loredo for her insightful comments on the very rough first draft, and for letting me play with her friendly (albeit projectile) cats on my time off; Tim Jarrell and Kris Kliemann for bringing CTW and Hyperion together as partners and for making this book possible; Anna Jane Hays for trusting the reins of the book to me and for guiding me in the right direction all along the way; Maureen O'Brien for her great objective eyes and artistic blue pencil marks; and most of all, Jen Koch for identifying the inner Muppet in me and having the faith to hire me as the author of this project, for her great editing and incredible support, advice, and guidance throughout the insane process of making this book, and for pushing hard to make this book as much fun as the show (well, almost, anyway).

Finally, of course, I have to thank my family: my mother and father for introducing me to *Sesame Street* some thirty years ago, and for indulging me when I wanted to EAT COOKIES! like Cookie Monster; my brother for allowing me to pester him more than Ernie ever did Bert; and of course, my wife Suzanne, who endured my Grover, Kermit, and Cookie imitations, my constant *Sesame Street* singing, and endless tape-watching as this book was coming together. I love you more than Bert loves pigeons.

All of the scripts, sketches, and quotes in this book were taken directly from scripts and transcripts of the original shows on which they aired, and this book wouldn't be complete if we didn't acknowledge the creators of this writing. *Sesame Street* has been written for the past 30 years by an incredibly talented group of writers who wrote life into classic characters and brought life to new ones. Their words and wisdom have made us laugh and learn, and will do so for many generations to come. Many thanks to this stellar group for their incredible canon of work:
Joe Bailey, Gary Belkin, Lou Berger, John Boni, Molly Boylan, Christian Clark, Sara Compton, Tom Dunsmuir, Annie Evans, Christine Ferraro, Judy Freudberg, Peggy Fulton, Lloyd Garver, Tony Geiss, John Glines, Denise James, Ian James, David Johnson, Jerry Juhl, Bo Kaprall, Robert Kelly, Emily Perl Kingsley, David Korr, Nina Link, Sonia Manzano, Joseph Mazzarino, Michael McCarthy, Jeff Moss, Marty Nadler, Bob Oksner, Ross Parker, Michael Preminger, Matt Robinson, Adam Rudman, Mark Saltzman, Nancy Sans, Luis Santeiro, Josh Selig, Ray Sipherd, Jocelyn Stevenson, Norman Stiles, Jon Stone, Peter Swet, Cathi Rosenberg-Turow, Belinda Ward, John Weidman, Dan Wilcox, Mo Willems, Mark Zelenovich, Paul Zimmerman.

For their cooperation: Tony Bennett, Johnny Cash, Ray Charles, Ellen DeGeneres, Danny DeVito, Phil Donahue, Roger Ebert, Jodie Foster, Mel Gibson, Whoopi Goldberg, John Goodman, James Earl Jones, Bo Jackson, Ziggy Marley, Itzhak Perlman, David Robinson, Fred Rogers, Linda Ronstadt, Gene Siskel, Susan Sarandon, Paul Simon, James Taylor, Barbara Walters, Noah Wyle, and Rosie O'Donnell.

—David Borgenicht

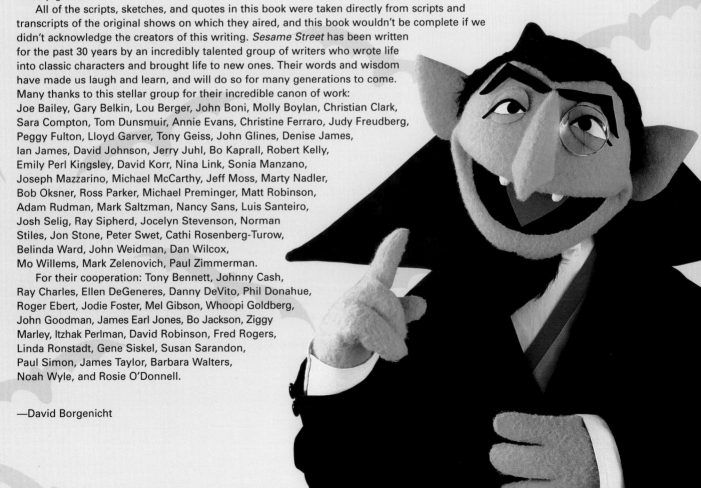

# CONTENTS

# FOREWORD

*Sesame Street* became the most famous street in America in one television season. This book has been thirty years in the making. It represents the efforts of thousands of people who have helped to make *Sesame Street* a cultural, educational, and media phenomenon.

But none of us had any idea how far we were going.

Thirty years ago, none of us had any idea that *Sesame Street* and the Children's Television Workshop would grow into the international institutions that they are today. None of us had any idea that the characters we were creating would become pop-culture icons. They were simply good vehicles for teaching children numbers, letters, and cognitive concepts. None of us knew we were creating a show that would win seventy-one Emmys and eight Grammys. None of us knew we were building a family that every child watching would feel a part of.

Our original goal was simple: to create a successful television program that would make a difference in the lives of children, in particular, poor inner-city children, and help prepare them for school. That goal might seem simple in retrospect, but at the time it was a revolutionary concept. In the late 1960s the use of television as an educational tool was unproven. We knew that young children watched a great deal of television in the years before they went to school. We knew also that they liked cartoons, game shows, and situation comedies; that they responded to slapstick humor and music with a beat; and above all, that they were attracted by fast-paced, highly visual, oft-repeated commercials.

We thought that, perhaps, if we created an educational show that capitalized on some of commercial television's most engaging traits (its slick production, its sophisticated writing, and quality film and animation work), we just might find a way to make this "preschool educational television program" work. The wasteland of children's programming was too vast for a major effort not to attract at least some attention and audience. We had a good idea, and we thought it would work.

From the beginning, we—the planners of the project—designed the show as an experimental research project with educational advisors, researchers, and television producers collaborating as equal partners.

That partnership is what has made *Sesame Street* unique. Writers, producers, directors, researchers, and performers all work together with a clear goal in mind, and we work hard to find the best path to that goal.

Without the research, *Sesame Street* would have been just another kiddie show. But the same can be said of any of the significant components of the show's success. What if Jim Henson and his team hadn't created such wonderful characters? What if Joe Raposo and Jeff Moss hadn't written *Sesame Street*'s memorable, timeless music? What if the show's wonderful writers, researchers, educators, directors, and producers hadn't devoted themselves to making *Sesame Street* so special?

Thankfully, we'll never know, because they all *did* contribute, joining forces to make a show that has changed children's television, and managed to do some good along the way. The show is still a phenomenon to this day, a phenomenon that shows no signs of flagging. I fully expect that someday thirty years from now the children and grandchildren of today's viewers will be sitting at the kitchen table, humming "People in Your Neighborhood" and "Rubber Duckie." And the world will be humming along with them.

—Joan Ganz Cooney, 1998

# INTRODUCTION

There is an old Ernie and Bert routine in which Ernie is standing in the living room of their basement apartment, holding a banana in his ear.

"Ernie, why do you have that banana in your ear?" Bert asks him.

"To keep the alligators away," Ernie answers.

"Er-nie," says Bert, "There are no alligators on *Sesame Street*!"

"Works pretty good, doesn't it, Bert?" Ernie replies.

Well, it's worked for thirty years.

*Sesame Street* isn't just a TV show—it's a very special place. It's a place we went to play and learn every day, a place we went to see family and friends, a place we went where monsters, animals, numbers, letters, and humans of every size, shape, and color lived together and shared in the joys and sorrows and laughter of life.

This book is a true fan's guide to the show—a scrapbook of thirty hysterical, remarkable, wonderful years that brings it all back. Within these pages are the classic moments we all remember, shared generational memories we can now relive through pictures, scripts, and songs—a yearbook of all our favorite characters, classic bits like "Near and Far," "Monsterpiece Theater," and "*Sesame Street* News," wild parodies and absurd gameshows, and the lyrics to timeless songs like "Sing," "Bein' Green," and "Rubber Duckie." In this book you'll rediscover the show again through character profiles, quotes and anecdotes, in-depth looks at key cast members and performers, never before revealed information (like what the Muppets first looked like—you won't believe it), behind-the-scenes stories, incredible trivia, and lots of other *Sesame Street* surprises.

So enjoy your trip back to the street of your youth, back to where Big Bird nests, where Oscar grouches, where Bob and Linda, Luis and Maria, Gordon and Susan, and all the rest sing, dance, teach, and tell stories. Back to the place where there are definitely no alligators.

—David Borgenicht, 1998

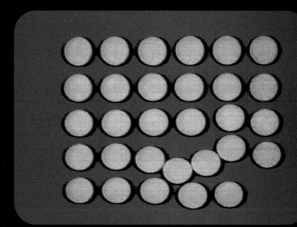

chapter one

# Can You Tell Me How We Got to Sesame Street?

**The *Sesame Street* Story**

*All I need is some beaks, some feathers, and a curriculum.*
—Big Bird

*In 1968 we didn't know what we were getting into... we didn't know that television could teach. ... It hadn't been done before.*
—Gerry Lesser, original *Sesame Street* director of curriculum

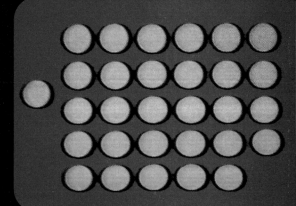

It 's 9:01 in the morning. Sunlight beats down on you as you lie in the top bunk of your bunk bed. You're a little uncomfortable in your superhero feetie pajamas, but you don't mind. It's time for your favorite show—time for *Sesame Street* (or "Sesameet," as your two-year-old brother would say). You wipe the sleep from your eyes and pad off to the TV room. You drag the beanbag chair across the room and sit way too close to the TV. You reach up and turn the set on—it's a small, remoteless black-and-white number with aluminum foil on the rabbit ears. As the little white dot grows into a bright, vibrant picture, you hear it—it's that song! "Sun-ny day, sweepin' the clouds away...." You smile. A big yellow bird waves for you to come along, to come and play with them all, to go to where the air is sweet. And so you do. Life, you think, is good.

**YOU KNOW YOU'RE OVER THIRTY WHEN YOU REMEMBER...**
The thirty dots that counted their way down the screen in between sketches

Despite what some kids thought back in the 1960s, *Sesame Street* wasn't always around. In fact, before 1969, nothing like it had ever been seen. Luckily, nice people like the letters W and S and the numbers 2 and 3, the Corporation for Public Broadcasting, and the Ford Foundation stepped up to the plate to sponsor a show that would change the face of children's television and the way children learned.

*Sesame Street* was made possible by the tireless efforts of many visionaries—brilliant producers, researchers, writers, directors, musicians, designers, performers—and television commercials.

That's right—TV commercials helped make *Sesame Street* possible. They didn't pay for the show; in fact, *Sesame Street* was never supposed to be commercially oriented. But anyone who knows what to do in Nikes, what your bologna's first name is, and what *not* to do with the Charmin, knows the power of commercials. But you probably don't know that the rapid-fire pace, slick production, and catchy music of television commercials inspired *Sesame Street*'s unique look and appeal. Just before the first show aired, Joan Ganz Cooney, the founding mother of *Sesame Street*, described this premise in the *New York Times*: "Traditional educators may not be nuts about this, but we're going to clip along at a much faster pace than anyone's used to in children's programs. [Kids] like commercials and banana-peel humor and avant-garde video and audio techniques....We have to infuse our content into forms children find accessible."

Could a television show do for letters, numbers, and educational concepts what commercials were doing for deodorants, canned foods, and cleaning products? Hey, it was so crazy, it just might work.

In the early 1960s, America was watching *Gilligan's Island*, *Gomer Pyle, U.S.M.C.*, *My Favorite Martian*, and *Mission: Impossible*. The most intellectual prime-time program was *What's My Line?*

But in 1966, Ms. Cooney had another idea. As a young television documentary producer, her primary focus was the political and social issues of the day. Although she had never worked on educational or children's programming, she believed in its potential and set out to blaze a new trail.

After extensive research, and with empirical data on her side, Ms. Cooney sowed the seeds of The Children's Television Workshop—and its longest running and most influential creation, *Sesame Street*. If she hadn't, generations of children would have had to learn to count by logging the number of times Gilligan *almost* got off the island, or the number of times Jeannie *almost* got her master's wishes right.

**When people ask for a thumbnail sketch of what *Sesame Street* is, I always say it's a comedy show that teaches. We have the best comedy writers on TV working for us. That's why it works.**

—Arlene Sherman, supervising producer of *Sesame Street*

---

**W**
Has sponsored show more than: 120 times
Has stood for: Wand, Wanda the Witch, West, Worm, Water, Wave

---

## *SESAME STREET*'S FOUR ORIGINAL EDUCATIONAL OBJECTIVES WERE TO TEACH KIDS:

**SYMBOLIC REPRESENTATION**
Learning letters, numbers, and shapes—what they look like, how to say them, and how they are used. In the first season, counting was limited to the numbers one through ten.

**COGNITIVE PROCESSES**
Developing reasoning and problem-solving skills—like matching and sorting objects into groups, or predicting what will happen next in a series of events—as well as understanding more relational concepts like fast/slow and above/below.

**PHYSICAL ENVIRONMENT**
Discovering cycles that occur in nature and identifying living things; also determining how man-made objects relate to the natural world.

**SOCIAL ENVIRONMENT**
Learning about the community of family, home, and neighborhood, and how people may have different ways of experiencing and seeing things. Also, addressing social interactions such as cooperation and conflict resolution, and social issues like cultural diversity.

---

**I want this show to jump and move fast and feel and sound like 1969, because kids are turned on visually!**
—Joan Ganz Cooney, 1969, the year *Sesame Street* began

## THE RIGHT STUFF

The skies on *Sesame Street* have always been sunny, thanks to the creative writers, researchers, producers, and other talented people that were found in those very early start-up years. With perseverance and a lot of luck, Ms. Cooney and her colleagues sought out a small group of people with all the right stuff—people that have helped to make *Sesame Street* the cultural and educational phenomenon it is today:

### THE DREAM TEAM

**Dave Connell**, vice president and executive producer, credited the show's success to "this mystical business of being in the right place at the right time."

**Samuel Gibbon**, the show's producer, remembers: "The notion that maybe it was time to do something useful was pretty overpowering."

**Jon Stone**, the producer and director of the show for more than twenty-six years and the man largely responsible for the tone and style of the show, said that the creators "didn't want another clubhouse or treasure house or tree-house... my proposal was that this should be a real inner-city street, and we should populate it with real people."

**Jeff Moss**, a talented young writer, joined the team after a few weeks of scripts had already been written by Jon Stone and Joe Raposo. He says now, "I'm old enough to know what a once-in-a-lifetime thing is, and *Sesame Street* is a once-in-a-lifetime thing."

**Jim Henson**, the creative genius who gave us Kermit, Grover, and the rest of the Muppets, once said that "we can use television and film to be an influence for good; and... we can help to shape the thoughts of children and adults in a positive way."

**Joe Raposo**, a talented musician and composer, was hired to oversee *Sesame*'s music. He wrote the famous songs "Sing" and "Bein' Green," and once explained that *Sesame Street*'s songs didn't talk down to kids; his philosophy was "we're just dealing with a very short audience."

> I used to say to the writers, "You've got two jobs: One is to do a television show that a four-year-old wants to watch. The second is to do a show that *you* want to watch."
> —Jeff Moss, former head writer

## NOT EXACTLY THE CASTING COUCH

The original cast first consisted only of Bob, Susan, Gordon, and Mr. Hooper, and real-life kids from local elementary schools (usually from disadvantaged neighborhoods) who came on from time to time. But why did all of the preschoolers love and trust them so much? Because they weren't chosen by a Hollywood casting agent with a cell phone, but by children themselves. The large group of potential cast members was whittled down by a group of actual schoolchildren. The actors who got the most enthusiastic thumbs-up from the kids were the ones ultimately selected to be on the show.

> Loretta Long, who plays Susan, remembers that at her audition she wasn't prepared to sing but when she had to, she stood in front of the camera and, as she recalls, "in the best Baptist tradition," accompanied herself with claps as she sang "I'm a Little Teapot." She was later told when the kids saw her test, they leapt up and sang along with her.

## WHO WAS MISSING ON THE STREET? THE MUPPETS, OF COURSE!

Initially, *Sesame Street*'s creators didn't plan to include Muppets on the *Street*. The Muppets were to appear only in taped inserts *between* street segments, animations, and films. But during the pilot testing, researchers discovered that the children lost interest during the street segments, and only paid attention when the Muppets and animations were on.

"We didn't plan to have Muppets on the street interacting with the human cast members because we thought that would confuse the children," Ms. Cooney remembers. "But we decided that was nonsense." So Big Bird and Oscar made their New York debuts as the first two *Sesame Street* Muppets.

The characters of Big Bird, Ernie, Bert, and other Muppets not only were created to entertain, but also to fill the curriculum needs that the researchers had pinpointed. Big Bird was to be the surrogate child, a somewhat goofy, clumsy character who questioned the same things that children at home might question. Ernie was a funny, mischievous character who would teach basic reasoning and logic (or illogic, as the case may be). His best friend, Bert, was the more serious partner who would keep Ernie in check, and act as the good-natured fall guy. And Oscar the Grouch was intended to help kids learn about their positive and negative emotions, and to learn that feelings like anger and grouchiness were natural, and not always bad.

### AND THEY SAY IT'S ALL DOWNHILL AFTER THIRTY...

It's not easy being on the air for thirty years. Not many other shows have done it, but here are the few that have also reached the ripe old age of thirty:

*Meet the Press* (1947)
*The Today Show* (1952)
*Guiding Light* (1952)
*The Tonight Show* (1954)
*As the World Turns* (1956)
*ABC's Wide World of Sports* (1961)
*General Hospital* (1963)
*Days of Our Lives* (1965)
*One Life to Live* (1968)
*60 Minutes* (1968)
*Mr. Rogers' Neighborhood* (1968)

### FAMOUS FIRSTS

The first show was sponsored by the letters W, S, E, and the numbers 2 and 3. In reality, the show was made possible by grants from the Carnegie Corporation, the Corporation for Public Broadcasting, the Ford Foundation, Head Start, the Markle Foundation, the United States Office of Education, and the public television station WNET.

**E** Has sponsored show more than: 150 times
Has stood for:
Eat, Eel, Egg, Elephant, Enter, Exit

## MUPPET MAKEOVERS

When *Sesame Street* first aired, the look of the Muppets was still evolving. The street was pretty much as it would always be (it extended around the corner in 1993), but Big Bird didn't look the way he'd end up looking in a season or two.

He originally had very few feathers on top— and very little else up there, either. In fact, Big Bird came across as a bit more dim than the creators had originally

**Did You Know?** In Episode One, Big Bird was the first Muppet to appear on the show. Oscar was the second, and he uttered the following words: "Don't bang on my can! Go away."

intended. Thanks to designer Kermit Love, in Season Two, Big Bird was given a little extra plumage—a few more feathers in his cap and a lot more brain power.

During the first season, Oscar the Grouch had a couple of problems, too. For starters, he was a bright, somewhat toxic orange color. Moreover, the positioning of the can on the set meant that Caroll Spinney (who plays Oscar) had to work with his left hand, even though the Muppet was designed for his right. This made Oscar's mouth seem a bit skewed. For the second season, the set

placement was shifted so that Caroll could work Oscar with his right hand, and orange Oscar was replaced with the green Oscar we know and love today. The one element Oscar has retained over the years are his original grouchy eyebrows.

In the beginning, Grover was not yet a full-fledged character. Yes, there was a strangely Grover-esque gray-green monster who appeared from time to time (he would become blue later), but he wasn't yet our lovable Grover—he had almost the right face, and the cute little furry arms, but he had no adorable little legs.

### THIRTY YEARS LATER AND WE'RE STILL COUNTING!

✿ *Sesame Street* first aired on November 10, 1969.
✿ More than 3,785 episodes later, *Sesame Street* now gets new local, international productions in nineteen different countries (but is aired in more than 140) and is a full-fledged licensing, publishing, music, and media phenomenon.
✿ The Children's Television Workshop has published more than 600 *Sesame Street* books, and publishes six magazines with a monthly readership of more than twelve million children and adults.

✿ *Sesame Street* has hosted more than 250 celebrity guests.
✿ *Sesame Street* is shown several times daily on more than 300 PBS stations throughout the United States.
✿ Seventy-seven percent of American preschool children watch *Sesame Street* at least once a week. More than eleven million people (children and adults) watch the show in an average week.
✿ *Sesame Street* has won more than 100 awards: seventy-one Emmys (more than any show in history!);eight Grammys; two George Foster Peabody Awards; four Parents' Choice Awards; the Prix Jeunesse International; a Clio Award; and an Action for Children's Television Special Achievement Award, just to name a few.
✿ The show has already reared two generations of children, and it shows no signs of flagging. There are now more than seventy million *Sesame Street* alumni! All magna cum laude, of course.

**Did You Know?** Today, the creation of the show's Muppets is a collaborative effort between The Children's Television Workshop (who conceive the characters) and the versatile members of The Jim Henson Company (who design, construct, and bring the characters to life).

*Sesame Street* has become a part of our popular culture, a street we can all call home—in English, or Spanish, or Kuwaiti. It's a place where we can find our family and friends. It's the kind of place where, as former head writer Norman Stiles says, we all dream of going: "I'd love to live on *Sesame Street*. Everybody's good to everyone else—people deal with each other in a rational and caring way. They're having fun. They like learning. It's just a great place to be."

It isn't a *perfect* street, however. It's not a magical world in which everything is wonderful. The characters have faults, but they deal with them. They argue, but they make up. They make mistakes, but they fix them. They sometimes hurt each other's feelings, but never on purpose. They don't always make the right choices or do the right thing, but they always try harder the next time around. More than anything, they're every little kid in feetie pajamas and every grown-up who secretly sings "Rubber Duckie" in the shower.

Like life, *Sesame Street* is a place where dreams are real and attainable, and where things can get better when people pay attention to each other, themselves, and their community.

You've never seen a street like *Sesame Street*. Everything happens here. You're gonna love it!
—Gordon's first lines on the first show

## chapter two

# I Can't Hear You—I've Got a Banana in My Ear
## The Classic Moments

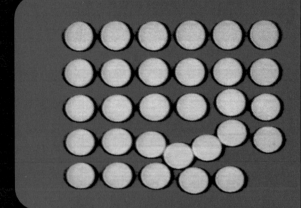

Hair is a part of you. It is not a part
of me, because I am a frog.
—Kermit

Anywhere I am is HERE.
Anywhere I am not is THERE.
—Grover

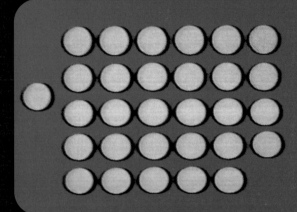

Ah, the canon of the classics.

Where would we all be without the Greek myths? The works of Shakespeare and Milton? The art of Rembrandt, Picasso, Michelangelo, and Monet? And of course, Grover's famous lecture on "Near" and "Far," the voluminous—and very classy—archives of Alastair Cookie's "Monsterpiece Theater," brilliant animations like "The King of 8" and "The Ladybug Picnic," or Kermit's legendary interviews with Rapunzel, Humpty Dumpty, and other fairy tale participants, to name only a few?

We'd be nowhere—particularly in this book. For these pages capture the classic *Sesame Street* moments and milestones over the years, moments like when Maria and Luis got married, when Snuffy became real, when Mr. Hooper died... moments that have stayed in viewers' minds forever. This is the *Sesame Street* canon—the masterpieces.

What follows are flashbacks, in the form of scripts, anecdotes, songs, and much more. Read the scripts out loud. Sing the old songs to your friends. Imitate the characters as you read. The voices will come back easily. In fact, you might find that they never really went away.

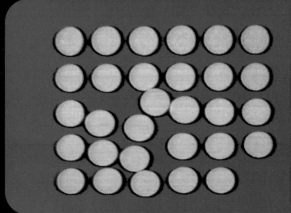

the importance of being

# Ernie & Bert

In all great friendships there is a yin and a yang. Abbott had Costello. Oscar had Felix. Thelma had Louise. And of course Ernie has Bert. And Bert has Ernie.

Pointy-headed, uni-browed, and banana-colored, Bert is analytical and responsible—the Felix Unger of the duo. When he's not playing checkers with his pigeon Bernice, Bert spends his days collecting bottle caps and paper clips, or being the butt of Ernie's jokes. He can usually be duped into getting the smallest piece of pizza and the shortest string of licorice. But Bert usually forgives Ernie; and occasionally he gets Ernie back for *his* tricks—usually by making Ernie clean their apartment. But not often.

Oval-headed, orange-colored, and perma-grinning Ernie is the trickster—the Oscar Madison, the free spirit—of the pair. Ernie spends his days and many nights, thinking about all kinds of things and keeping Bert awake—things like what it would be like to live on the moon, what might happen while he's at the zoo or in the bathtub, or why Bert's not home yet. It's clear he loves Bert, even though he delights in teasing him. Ernie's crafty and always finds a way to come out ahead, if only by a little. But it's always obvious that he values Bert's friendship immensely, and that he simply wouldn't know what to do

without his ol' buddy and best pal.

Sharing the basement apartment of 123 Sesame Street, these two eccentric roommates have taught us many valuable lessons over the years—how to share (sort of), how to cooperate (they try), what to do when you can't fall asleep (count things, loudly), and how to keep alligators away (you'll remember).

## THE BANANA SKETCH, PART I

**This is the "Who's on First" of Bert and Ernie bits.**

(Ernie is standing in the apartment humming to himself. He's holding a banana in his ear. Bert approaches.)

**Bert:** Hey Ernie? Hey, uh, Ern?

**Ernie:** (Notices Bert) Oh! Hi Bert!

**Bert:** Uh, yeah. Hey Ernie, uh, you know that you have a banana in your ear?

**Ernie:** (Loudly) What was that, Bert?

**Bert:** I said, you have a banana in your ear, Ernie. Uh, bananas are food. They are to eat, not to put in your ear, Ernie.

**Ernie:** (Loudly) Whatdya say, Bert?

**Bert:** (Yelling) WILL YOU JUST TAKE THAT BANANA OUTTA YOUR EAR!

**Ernie:** (Yelling back) I'M SORRY—YOU'LL HAVE TO SPEAK A LITTLE LOUDER, BERT! I CAN'T HEAR YOU! I HAVE A BANANA IN MY EAR!

(Bert rumples in anger.)

secret fact:
In 1997, 1.2 million Sing 'n' Snore Ernies were sold.

## WHAT WE'VE LEARNED FROM ERNIE AND BERT

❀ If you don't want to get cookie crumbs in your bed, eat the cookies in your best friend's bed.

❀ When you can't get to sleep, try counting sheep. If the sheep are too loud, try fire engines. If the fire engines are too loud, try popping balloons. If all else fails, dance yourself to sleep.

❀ Be careful when you sneeze or your nose might come off in the hanky.

❀ Pigeons are darn good dancers.

❀ It's okay to be boring.

## HOW TO TELL IF YOUR OLD BUDDY BERT IS ASLEEP

Ernie is a master of many things—procrastination, rationalization, and imagination, just to name a few. But more than anything, he's a master of the "accidental" wake up. Observe his most classic method—the "Poke-Poke" technique.

**Ernie:** Hey Ber-rt! Hey Bert! Old buddy Bert! Hey Bert! Where are you, Bert? *(Sees Bert sleeping)* Oh! Hmm. Gee. You know, it is just possible that my old buddy Bert here is asleep. For one thing, he's lying down, which he usually does when he is asleep. For another thing his eyes are closed. And for another thing, he's not answering me when I talk. So old buddy Bert is probably asleep. I will check just to make sure. *(Pokes him)* POKE POKE POKE POKE POKE POKE POKE! Note how I can poke old buddy Bert in the stomach and he doesn't complain. Now when old buddy Bert is awake and I poke him in the stomach, he complains. *(Lifts Bert's arm)* Oh, looky here. Note how floppy and soggylike old buddy Bert's arm is. Hmm. When old buddy Bert is awake he's not floppy and soggylike. So, I'm quite certain that old buddy Bert is very definitely asleep. *(Bert now wakes up, annoyed)* On the other hand, now his eyes are open! My old buddy Bert's eyes are usually open only when he is awake! So he's probably awake, but I will check just to make sure. *(Pokes him)* POKE POKE POKE POKE POKE POKE POKE!

**Bert:** ER-NIE! STOP IT!

**Ernie:** See! I was right! He is awake!

## WHEN YOUR RIGHT HAND DOESN'T KNOW WHAT YOUR LEFT HAND IS DOING

It takes two Muppeteers to work Ernie. One puts his right hand in Ernie's mouth and makes him speak. The other puts his right arm in Ernie's right arm. The "right-hand man" is the one who feeds the puppet most of the props and is the hand that performs most of the action.

I love pigeons more than

anything else in this world—

besides oatmeal. —Bert

I was never really happy with Bert's character until about a year in when I realized . . . that he was a very boring character, and I'd use that weakness as a strength for him.

—Frank Oz, who performs Bert

## SAT: SESAME ACHIEVEMENT TEST

*Starting to feel queasy? Well, sharpen those number two pencils and get your timers ready! If you want to graduate from Sesame Street U you'll need to pass this test. Throughout the book you'll encounter questions about the show that will test your Sesame Street Aptitude. Here's how you'll learn what kind of a fan you really are—whether you're a true "Sesamite" or simply a "Sesame Wanna-be."*

**ERNIE AND BERT WERE NAMED FOR THE POLICEMAN AND THE TAXICAB DRIVER IN *IT'S A WONDERFUL LIFE*.**

○ TRUE or ○ FALSE?

*Answer: False. Sesame writers insist that it's just a coincidence. Of course, we don't have to actually believe them.*

**WHEN ERNIE BROUGHT HOME A PUPPY, BERT WANTED TO NAME IT**

A ○ Godzilla the wonder dog
B ○ Bernice
C ○ Norman
D ○ Frank

*Answer: C. Possibly in honor of Norman Stiles, the head writer of the show at the time.*

**BERT: BERNICE AS**

A ○ The Brady Bunch : Tiger
B ○ Big Bird : Snuffy
C ○ Laverne: Shirley
D ○ Lucy : Rickie

*Answer: A. Bernice is Bert's pet pigeon, Tiger was the Bradys' dog.*

**BERT IS _____ THAN ERNIE.**

A ○ taller
B ○ yellower
C ○ duller
D ○ pointier
E ○ all of the above

*Answer: E*

**pssst!!**

## secret fact:
### How Ernie Got His Stripes

In case you never noticed, both Ernie and Bert wear striped shirts. However, Ernie's stripes run horizontally, which makes him look more relaxed. Bert's run vertically, which makes him look more uptight. And we thought vertical stripes were merely slimming!

## HOW TO EVEN THINGS OUT, ACCORDING TO ERNIE

Ernie is a master of the friendly con. He can approach any situation and make sure that he gets the better deal—more cookies, more pizza, more grape juice—even though he makes it seem as if he's trying to even things out. Here's his technique.

1. Look at what it is that you have and determine who has more and who has less (curriculum *is* important, after all).

2. Tell Bert that you know how to fix things. Take the bigger slice of pizza or the bigger glass of juice. Eat or drink a little bit to make the portions equal. Realize that in your selfless attempt to even things out you have accidentally reversed the situation. The bigger slice or glass of juice is now smaller. But you can solve this.

3. Take another bite or sip of whatever is now bigger in order to "even things out again." Continue this charade until both pieces of pizza, both glasses of juice, or whatever are gone. Ignore Bert's complaints until he passes out on the floor.

## HOW TO EAT BERT'S COOKIES, ACCORDING TO ERNIE:

Ernie is the king of rationalizations. He possesses the uncanny ability to convince himself that "Bert won't mind" if he has a bite of this or that while Bert's not around. After all, isn't that what friends are for?

1. Look longingly at Bert's plate of five cookies.
2. Decide that Bert won't mind if you take a tiny bite of one cookie.
3. Take a tiny bite.
4. Realize that the cookie now doesn't look even—take another bite to "even it up."
5. Notice that now the cookie isn't round. Cookies should be round. Take another bite to achieve the perfect shape.
6. Now the cookie is round. But you notice that now it's too small—so eat the whole thing.
7. There are now only four cookies left. Maybe Bert won't remember how many there were.
8. Bert comes home. Bert remembers. He tells you how he was looking forward to eating his plate of "five cookies." He counts the cookies, and discovers that there are only four left.
9. Bert becomes angry. He tells you that he doesn't want four cookies.
10. Now is your chance. Innocently say: "You don't want four cookies?"
11. Bert will probably say, "I certainly don't, Ernie. If there's one thing I don't want it's four cookies."
12. Tell him that you can fix it so that there aren't four cookies anymore. Eat one more cookie and say, "Now there aren't four cookies anymore. There're three now."

## ERNIE'S SHORT STORY: "THE BEST SHORT STORY EVER WRITTEN"

**Ernie:** *(Dramatically)* A-B-C-D-E-F-G. Now comes the sad part, Bert. *(Sadly)* H-I-J-K-L-M-N-O-P. *(Sniffle)*

**Bert:** That's the alphabet, Ernie.

**Ernie:** *(Getting his composure)* Just a second, Bert. Now comes the action part.

**Bert:** 'Course.

**Ernie:** *(Excitedly)* Q-R-S-T-U-V! Now comes the big finish! W-X-Y... *(Long pause)*

**Bert:** Well?

**Ernie:** Well what, Bert?

**Bert:** Well finish it!

**Ernie:** What? And tell you how the story ends? Then you won't read it yourself, Bert!

### SOMETHING IS WRONG WITH THIS CHEESE

Ernie is looking at a plate with a chunk of Swiss cheese on it. He remarks to Bert, "Something is wrong with this cheese."

**Bert:** Cheese with holes in it tastes different from our regular cheese—it tastes better.

**Ernie:** You expect me to believe that—that cheese with holes in it tastes better?

**Bert:** Well, now look. See, it's the holes that make it taste better!

**Ernie:** Hmm. It's the holes, huh?

**Bert:** Yeah!

**Ernie:** I tell you what, Bert. I'll eat the cheese...

**Bert:** Yeah?

**Ernie:** And you eat the holes.

## THE ANGST OF ERNIE

You know, it gets pretty lonely around here without Bert....Gee—you don't suppose anything has happened to him, do you? Gee, that would be awful if anything happened to my old buddy Bert! Oh, maybe while he was walking home a whole group of monsters grabbed him and took him back to their cave....Ohhhh, that's scary, isn't it? Poor buddy Bert. In a cave with all those hairy scary monsters...that scares me to think about it. Hey, but maybe those monsters aren't scary at all, maybe they're nice and friendly monsters, and maybe they're having a party, and they invited Bert to the party and that's where he is now! (Angry) Now that isn't very nice, is it? Old buddy Bert at a party while I'm here all by myself...I don't like that at all. In fact, that makes me angry! Bert at a party. But oh, oh—what if Bert decides he likes those monsters better than he likes me, and he wants to stay and live with those monsters, and he'll never come home again! (Sad) Ohhh, I'll be all by myself and I'll never see my old buddy Bert again! (Crying)

### ERNIE

**BORN:** January 28 (Aquarius)
Like most Aquarians, Ernie seems innocent enough, but is full of mischief. Expect the unexpected with this Aquarian—like when he takes his bowling ball into the bathtub. He shares his sign with Alan Alda (who probably has his own rubber duckie), Lewis Carroll (who probably saw a few Twiddlebugs himself), and Gene Siskel (whose best friend just happens to be Roger E-BERT!).
**VOICE AND PUPPETRY:** Jim Henson (now Steve Whitmire)
**SCIENTIFIC NAME:** Duckius philicus
**QUOTE:** "Hey, Bert old buddy? Are you asleep?"
**PHILOSOPHY:** Do unto others before they can do unto you.
**FAVORITE SONGS:** "Rubber Duckie"; "You've Got a Friend"; "Bug the One You're With"
**BEST FRIEND:** Bert
**LIKES:** Playing tricks on Bert; eating Bert's pizza; taking baths with Rubber Duckie
**DISLIKES:** When it's his turn to clean up; when Bert won't play
**HOBBIES:** Imagining; thinking; playing word games, and (of course) tricking Bert.

Ernie: Are you mad, Bert?

Bert: Oh no, Ernie, I'm not mad.
Ernie: Oh, good, Bert. I just wasn't sure there for a second. Sometimes it's hard to tell.

## Not minding, that's what friends are for!
—Ernie on friendship

## ERNIE AND BERT'S TOP TEN SONGS

1. "Rubber Duckie"
2. "I Don't Want to Live on the Moon"
3. "Doin' the Pigeon"
4. "I Want to Hold Your Ear"
5. "Honker Duckie Dinger Jamboree"
6. "Put Down the Duckie"
7. "Imagination"
8. "That's What Friends Are For"
9. "Would You Like to Buy an O?"
10. "I'm Square"

**BERT**

**BORN:** July 26 (Leo) Like some Leos, Bert lives in the shadow of other more glamorous, popular people. But Leos tend to wrap themselves in their dignity and not worry about how others perceive them (that's why Bert gets such a kick from doing "The Pigeon"). He shares his sign with Mick Jagger (who, like Bert, can't get no satisfaction), Dorothy Hamill (who's done the pigeon on ice), and Napoleon Bonaparte (who, like Bert, had an inferiority complex).

**VOICE AND PUPPETRY:** Frank Oz

**SCIENTIFIC NAME:** Monotonous squabius

**QUOTE:** "Er-nie!"

**PHILOSOPHY:** Be patient—or you'll be a patient.

**FAVORITE SONGS:** "Doin' the Pigeon"; "You've Got a Friend"; "That's What Friends Are For"

**BEST FRIEND:** Ernie

**LIKES:** Ws; pigeons; brass band music; oatmeal; boring stories; watching weather forecasts on TV; argyle socks; the color gray

**DISLIKES:** When Ernie wakes him up with silly questions like "What are we going to do tomorrow?"

**HOBBIES/OBSESSION:** Collecting Figgy Fizz bottle caps, paper clips, and pink erasers

## do you remember?

❉ When Ernie made a sculpture of Bert, but didn't have enough clay to give him a nose—so he borrowed Bert's?

❉ When Ernie shows Bert that he has string on all his fingers, and that each string reminded him of a previous string, until the last finger, which "reminds me that we're all out of string. I have to go out and buy some more"?

❉ When Bert and Ernie were arguing because Ernie wouldn't turn the television down, so they had an appliance war and each of them turned on a different one—from the record player and the vacuum cleaner to the blender—more and more appliances to drown out the previous one until they blew a fuse?

❉ When Ernie used Bert's cowboy hat for a fishbowl?

❉ When Ernie and Bert were cavemen?

❉ When Ernie bought an invisible ice cream cone with an invisible nickel?

❉ When Ernie and Bert played the following game:
Ernie: I one the sandbox
Bert: I two the sandbox
And so on until Ernie gets Bert to say, "I eight the sandbox," and Ernie then asks, "How did it taste?"

❉ When Ernie has an "important note" for Bert, but can't remember where he put it or what it said? He thinks it might be in the clothes hamper and proceeds to throw all of the clothes out of the hamper to find the note, completely messing up the apartment. He finds the note at the bottom of the hamper. It reads, "Dear Bert, It's your turn to clean up the apartment. Love, Ernie."

## Bert's everybody's idea of a blind date.

—Arlene Sherman, supervising producer of *Sesame Street*

There's an art to being boring. Not everyone can do it well. Not everyone would prefer to sit around reading the newspaper front to back while his best friend plays games in the same room. Not everyone gets excited by protective raingear. But Bert does, and in doing so, he teaches us an important lesson—that the world is made up of all kinds of people, and we can love the boring ones, too.

## THE BERT AND ERNIE PERSONALITY QUIZ

Which member of this famous duo are you more like? Do you have a tendency to play tricks on your friends and to dream up all kinds of crazy scenarios, or would you rather sit at home reading your book of boring stories and playing checkers with Bernice, your pet pigeon? Take this simple test to find out.

**1. MY IDEA OF THE PERFECT DAY IS:**

a) sitting with a big bowl of oatmeal, reading the Pigeon News, and listening to marching band music.
b) playing with Rubber Duckie, and then pestering your best friend in new and exciting ways.

**2. I PREFER:**

a) vertical stripes.
b) horizontal stripes.

**3. MY IDEA OF THE PERFECT WOMAN IS:**

a) a stunning creature with a pointy head, a furry uni-brow, and a removable nose.
b) a fetching lass with an oval head, a perma-grin, and an infectious laugh.

**4. I'D LIKE TO VISIT:**

a) the Annual Paper Clip Collectors Convention and the National Association of W Lovers.
b) the moon.

**5. WHEN SOMETHING GOES WRONG, I:**

a) get really, really worked up, scream at the top of my lungs, and faint.
b) wake up my best friend to tell him about it.

**6. WHEN I CAN'T GET TO SLEEP, I:**

a) dream about pigeons ice-skating.
b) count sheep, dance, and wake up my best friend.

**7. MY IDEA OF THE PERFECT JOB IS TO BE A:**

a) curator at a Bottle Cap Museum.
b) professional Practical Joker.

**8. WHICH STATEMENT IS MOST LIKE YOU?**

a) "I can tell you, nothing beats sitting in my big comfortable chair and watching the weather forecast on TV."
b) "Rubber Duckie—you're the one."

**SCORING: If you have more than four (a)s:** your personality is pretty darn close to Bert's—a scary thought to some, but hey, it takes all kinds. Strike up the marching band music and do the pigeon.

**If you have more than four (b)s:** your personality is very like Ernie's, but as long as you keep it all in perspective, everything will be okay. Just keep your Rubber Duckie (and your bowling ball) close at hand.

# The King of 8

**O**nce upon a
time in the land of 8

There stood a castle very great.

And 8 flags waved in the air

For the King of 8 had put them there.

"I'm the King of 8, and I'm here to state

That everything here has to total 8.

The guards, for instance, by the gate

Must always number exactly 8."

# 1, 2, 3, 4, 5, 6, 7, 8

"In my castle in back of me are 8

Windows, you can see."

# 1, 2, 3, 4, 5, 6, 7, 8

"In those windows are my daughters,
Show yourselves, my dears!"

# 1, 2, 3, 4, 5, 6, 7, 8

"Each daughter has a silver crown with 8
Jewels going 'round."

# 1, 2, 3, 4, 5, 6, 7, 8

"So I love 8, 8 is great, 8 is the
number I do not—"

# WAIT!

Important news comes from the Queen—
A new baby! And I have seen

That she is well and doing fine!

"Good grief! It's Princess Number **9**!"

It's really thrilling for me that Big Bird is an important part of childhood for so many children. It's sort of like I grew up to be Mickey Mouse.

—Caroll Spinney,
Muppeteer for Big Bird

# BIG BIRD

## our fine feathered friend

In a funny way, everyone is like Big Bird.

That's not to say that we're all eight-foot-two-inch tall yellow birds with slightly quirky outlooks on the world, or that we sleep in nests the size of a Volkswagen bug, or that our best friend is a furry pachydermish giant—but hey, you never know.

Viewers really *identified* with Big Bird. He was the child on-screen, the viewers' six-year-old guide to the *Sesame Street* world. He asked all the questions kids wanted to ask, he experienced all the things kids were experiencing at the same time, and he learned as they did. Big Bird is the everychild of *Sesame Street*.

Big Bird wasn't always an innocent child. In the first season, the show's writers hadn't found his—well, his "Big Bird-ness" yet. During the first season Big Bird was like a dopey giant walkaround puppet. Eventually, however, the writers discovered what we the viewers always knew: Big Bird isn't stupid, he's just a big (very big) kid. He's also a guileless (and, coincidentally, flightless) bird who experiences the world innocently, and questions *everything*.

He feels what kids feel, and vice versa. In the same way that Big Bird tries to emulate others, kids try to emulate him (let's face it—we're all Birdketeers when you get down to it).

Through Big Bird, kids everywhere have experienced deep friendship (Snuffy), great loss (Mr. Hooper), and of course the extreme pleasures of a birdseed milkshake (shaken, not stirred).

Here are some of our fine feathered friend's most memorable moments.

### secret fact:

The role of Big Bird was originally offered to Frank Oz. Frank already had the full-body-costume puppet experience in the 1960s, while playing the La Choy dragon in a series of commercials that Jim Henson produced. The dragon suit was made almost entirely of rubber, and the dragon shot a flame from his mouth. Frank didn't really like the heat or the confinement of the experience. So no one was surprised when he passed on the Bird.

## WHAT'S IN BIG BIRD'S NEST AREA

A bubble-gum dispenser

A clock with no hands

A feather duster

A football helmet

A golf bag with one club

A hurricane lamp

A megaphone

A picture of Mr. Hooper

A Roman bust

A tricycle wheel

A watering can

An old record player

An umbrella

A mailbox

Snowshoes

## ON BIRD'S BOOKSHELF:

(actual titles) *March of Democracy, Shattered Lamp, Principles of Chemistry, Preface to Philosophy*

Who is a friend right till the end? Who has wings and even sings? Who's got the biggest beak you know? Who's got feathers head to toe? Who's the fella who's all yella?

—Big Bird

**BORN:** March 20 (Pisces)
Like all Pisceans, Big Bird is creative and artistic, and sees the world through rose-colored (or maybe yellow-colored) glasses. He shares his sign with Mr. Rogers (makes sense), Albert Einstein (it's all relative), and Spike Lee (go figure).
**VOICE AND PUPPETRY:** Caroll Spinney
**SCIENTIFIC NAME:** Bigus canarius
**HEIGHT:** 8' 2"
**QUOTE:** "Gee Mr. Looper! I mean Cooper! I mean Hooper!"
**PHILOSOPHY:** There's no such thing as a stupid question.
**FAVORITE SONGS:** "ABC-DEF-GHI"; "Freebird"; "A Wing and a Prayer"
**BEST FRIEND:** Snuffleupagus
**LIKES:** Figuring things out; being a part of everything; rollerskating; birdseed milkshakes from Mr. Hooper's store.
**Dislikes:** When he can't help; when nobody believes his best friend exists; chicken soup
**Hobbies:** Drawing pictures and writing poetry

## do you remember?

❧ Big Bird and the Birdketeers? (Oscar wouldn't let Big Bird join his Grouchkateer club, so Big Bird started his own club.)

❧ When Big Bird and Snuffy did the laundry with Savion Glover, but Snuffy couldn't fit into the laundry room?

❧ When Big Bird taught Snuffy how to skate in Central Park?

❧ When Gordon put Big Bird in charge of watching over the painting he'd just finished of *Sesame Street*? Big Bird was so concerned about protecting it that he made a "Wet Paint" sign and hung it directly on the painting—smearing Gordon's masterpiece beyond repair!

## SAT: SESAME ACHIEVEMENT TEST (BIG BIRD COMPREHENSION)

**BIG BIRD'S TEDDY BEAR IS NAMED FOR A CHARACTER ON** *M*A*S*H.* **HIS NAME IS:**

A ○ Trapper
B ○ Radar
C ○ Hot Lips
D ○ Hawkeye
E ○ Frank

*Answer: B. Caroll Spinney met Gary Burghoff, who played Radar, on The Hollywood Squares, and decided to name Big Bird's teddy bear in his honor.*

**WHO GAVE BIG BIRD HIS TEDDY BEAR?**

A ○ Mr. Handford
B ○ Snuffy
C ○ Buffy
D ○ Mr. Hooper

*Answer: D. It was a special gift.*

**FRANK SINATRA : JOHN F. KENNEDY AS**

A ○ Big Bird : Pat Nixon
B ○ Snuffy : Betty Ford
C ○ Kermit : Dan Quayle
D ○ Elmo: Bill Clinton

*Answer: A. Big Bird was invited to the White House by Pat Nixon, Sinatra was invited by Kennedy.*

**WHO JUDGED "THE BIG RACE" BETWEEN SNUFFY AND BIG BIRD?**

A ○ Mr. Rogers
B ○ Bryant Gumbel
C ○ Marv Albert
D ○ Bo Jackson

*Answer: A. When he was on the show, Mr. Rogers judged a running race in Central Park between Big Bird and Snuffy—but Snuffy didn't believe Mr. Rogers was ever really there.*

**Did You Know?** Even though all the Sesame Street Muppets are technically ageless, Big Bird is psychologically written to represent a six-year-old.

### BIG BIRD MEETS LITTLE BIRD

**Big Bird:** What are you?

**Little Bird:** I'm a bird, silly.

**Big Bird:** A bird? You're not a bird. I'm a bird. Birds are big.

**Little Bird:** Well, I'm a little bird.

**Big Bird:** You're sure?

**Little Bird:** Uh-huh.

**Big Bird:** Umph. I don't think you're a bird at all.

**Little Bird:** Well, look. Do you have a beak?

**Big Bird:** Well, of course I have a beak.

**Little Bird:** Well, so do I.... Do you have wings?

**Big Bird:** Well, yes, I'm a bird. Birds have wings.

**Little Bird:** Well, so do I.... Do you have feathers?

**Big Bird:** Sure! I'm covered with them! I'm a bird. Look at you! You've got feathers all over you, too. Why, you are a bird!

**Little Bird:** Yeah, I told you I was.

**Big Bird:** Well... a little bird.

**Little Bird:** Yeah, and you're a great big bird.

**Big Bird:** A big bird and a little bird. Can we be friends?

**Little Bird:** Yeah, I guess so.

> As a kid I was the smallest person in class—so it's really something to play the tallest person on TV.
> —Caroll Spinney

### THE BIRD IS BUGGED

When *Sesame Street* took a trip to the White House to visit Pat Nixon, the Secret Service's radio frequency got mixed up with Big Bird's microphone frequency—so the Secret Service was picking up the Bird's lines on their earpieces.

## BIG BIRD'S ODE TO HIMSELF

One day, Maria told Big Bird that if you're very close to someone, it's nice to write that person a poem or a song. Big Bird, as always, took that information to heart, and decided to write a poem to the person he's closest to: "Me!"

### ODE TO ME
by Big Bird

WHO LOOKS EXACTLY THE WAY THAT I LOOK?
ME!
WHEN I'M READING WHO'S HOLDING THE BOOK?
ME!
WHEN I WANT DINNER WHO WILL FEED ME?
ME!

WHO'S ALWAYS HANDY WHENEVER I NEED ME?
ME!
WHO IS A BIRD WHO IS HAPPY AND PROUD?
ME!
WHO IS A BIRD WHO STANDS OUT IN A CROWD?
ME!
WHO MAKES ME DANCE WHEN THE MUSIC IS JIVY?
WHO DO I SCRATCH WHEN I HAVE POISON IVY?
ME!

## BIG BIRD IMAGINES HE'S SHORT

**Big Bird:** Mr. Looper, I've been thinking.

**Mr. Hooper:** You have?

**Big Bird:** Yeah, I've been thinking—I'm kind of tall. Have you noticed that? I bet I'm the tallest person on *Sesame Street.*

**Mr. Hooper:** I bet you are.

**Big Bird:** Mr. Dooper, I was thinking… I like to imagine things. I'd like to imagine what it would be like to be short. A real tiny person—small enough to walk around on your counter…. *(Big Bird actually shrinks down and is now standing on Hooper's counter)* I'm imagining I'm so short I'm on Mr. Looper's counter. Let me look over the edge. *(Walks to the edge and peers over)* It's a long way to the floor. I'd hate to fall off now that I'm so little. I'm so little I could hide behind that soda pop bottle. *(Hooper begins to sponge the counter, almost knocking Big Bird off)* Mr. Booper doesn't even see me, I'm so little. I was afraid he was going to mop me right off. *(Approaches a rubber duckie on the counter)* Hey, Rubber Duckie! You're just the right size for me to be friends with you. This is fun! But I think it's better to be like I usually am—big, tall—so I think I'll imagine myself big again. Here I go. There. Wow. That was fun!

## THE QUOTABLE BIRD

I guess it's better to be who you are. Turns out people like you best that way, anyway.
—Big Bird

I'm too tall to be short.
—Big Bird

# Snuffy and Bird:

## you've got to have friends

The friendship between Big Bird and Mr. Snuffleupagus is irrefutable proof of the enduring power of love and companionship. (And yes, that's how you spell it—S-N-U-F-F-L-E-U-P-A-G-U-S. It's not "Snuffleufalgus" or "Snuppleupagus" or anything else.) It also happens to be ridiculous to see a huge yellow bird and a huge furry pachyderm-esque creature playing—even roller-skating!—together. But it's a beautiful thing.

Against all odds, Big Bird always insisted that his friend Snuffy *wasn't* imaginary, and in so doing he showed that he believed in his best friend and ultimately in the power of friendship. Together, as friends, they knew the scoop. Snuffy wasn't imaginary—he just had bad timing!

Watching the show between 1971 and 1985 (Snuffy's Invisible Years), viewers held their breaths each time Big Bird and Snuffy were together. Would the power of friendship win out this time? Would Bob, or Maria, or Luis *finally* see that Big Bird hadn't simply eaten some bad birdseed? Would Snuffy become an accepted member of the *Sesame Street* family?

The Big Bird/Snuffleupagus conspiracy played out for years longer than most other television conspiracies or soap operas—much longer than *The Fugitive* or *The X-Files*, for example. Finally, in 1985, Snuffy was seen for the first time by the *Sesame Street* neighborhood.

Since then, Snuffy's and Big Bird's friendship has been out in the open. And they've proven to us all that, no matter what, if you believe in yourself and in your friends, eventually everyone else will believe, too.

## KEEPING THE FAITH WASN'T ALWAYS EASY

**Big Bird:** *(Describing Snuffy to Rafael, Susan, and Gordon)*...And he has big legs and a real long twirly nose, and you'll really like him— *(Looking around)* Where'd he go? Mr. Snuffleupagus, where are you?

**Gordon:** *(Skeptical)* A Snuffleupagus, Big Bird?

**Big Bird:** Sure!

**Susan:** *(Also skeptical)* With big legs...?

**Rafael:** *(Also skeptical)*...And a long, twirly nose?

**Big Bird:** Sure! (Feeling their doubt) You—you believe me, don't you?

**Gordon:** Big Bird, I don't know how to say this, but I think you've been imagining things.

**Susan:** Big Bird, we've never even heard of a Snuffleupagus.

**Big Bird:** But—

**Rafael:** If he comes back, Big Bird, you let us know, Okay? *(They all say good-bye and leave)*

**Big Bird:** *(To camera)* They didn't believe me! You saw him, didn't you? Oh Mr. Snuffleupagus, where did you go?

### IT TAKES TWO: HOW SNUFFY WORKS

Martin Robinson, who speaks and manipulates the head for Snuffy, stands completely upright inside the head of the puppet, which is built on a rattan framework and is attached to Martin's waist with a Steadicam backpack. He navigates through use of a monitor inside the head. Martin's legs are in the two front legs, his left hand works the mouth, and his right hand works both eyes and the curved stick that works Snuffy's snuffle. In the back of Snuffy, Bryant Young has to hunch over to support Snuffy's back and to walk correctly.

### SAT: SESAME ACHIEVEMENT TEST (SNUFFLEUPASECTION)

**ON "SNUFFLEUPAGUS-AMERICAN DAY," SNUFFLEUPAGUSES:**

A ○ Dress in grass skirts
B ○ Dance the snuffle-hula
C ○ Celebrate their Hawaiian heritage
D ○ March in a parade
E ○ All of the above

*Answer: E. Snuffy and Alice celebrated the day together.*

**Did You Know?** Mr. Snuffleupagus is written to represent the psychological age of a four-year-old. He's seven feet tall, from the floor to the top of his head, and twelve feet long. Big for his age, isn't he?

**Mr. Snuffleupagus:** *Are you sure we met?*
**Big Bird:** *Well, pretty sure—after all, if we didn't meet, how would we know each other?*

**pssst!!**

secret fact:

*Sesame Street* once taped an episode in which Big Bird and Snuffy said good-bye to each other. Big Bird was finally convinced by the adults that Snuffy was imaginary. So he told Snuffy that they couldn't be friends anymore. Snuffy didn't understand. He said that he didn't feel imaginary, but he acknowledged that the grown-ups were smarter than he was and if they said he was imaginary, he must be. So Big Bird and Snuffy said good-bye. They told each other that they'd miss each other a lot, and hugged for one last time.

Then Big Bird noticed that Snuffy was crying, and that his tears were real! Bird realized that if Snuffy's tears were real, then he must also be real—which meant that they *could* be friends! He told Snuffy that they'd be friends forever.

After shooting the scene, the actors took the costumes off, and Jerry Nelson (who performed Snuffy at the time) and Caroll Spinney (Big Bird) discovered that while they were doing the scene, they had both been crying inside their costumes.

## WHERE WERE YOU WHEN GORDON, SUSAN, BOB, MARIA, AND LUIS SAW SNUFFY?

Do you remember where you were when the grown-ups *finally* saw Snuffleupagus? If you missed that moment, either because you were at school, or too old, or (gasp!) watching some other show, you can relive it right here, right now. Just don't blink, or you might miss it again.

*(Snuffy and Big Bird are in an excited conversation in the nest area, when they both notice that the camera [the viewer, really] is watching them. They talk to the camera.)*

**Snuffy:** Big Bird was just telling me that something that's never happened before on *Sesame Street* is going to happen *today*. What is it, Bird?

**Big Bird:** *(Importantly)* Today is the day that everybody on *Sesame Street* is finally going to meet you face to face!

**Snuffy:** *(Incredulous)* No!

**Big Bird:** *Yes!* Each and every grown-up who never believed you were real... just my imaginary friend... is gonna see you in the flesh—or rather, fur.

**Snuffy:** *NO!*

**Big Bird:** *YES!* After today I will never again hear them say, *"Oh, Mr. Snuffleupagus! Your imaginary friend."* Do you have any idea how many times I've heard that?

**Snuffy:** No.

**Big Bird:** Millions—maybe billions and billions. All that's over today, because *(mysterious music)* I have a plan. This is how it works. I'm here with you, and at the right moment I yell a secret word real loud and all the grown-ups hear it— and they come running out from wherever they are, and they see you and meet you!

**Snuffy:** Oh, wow! That is a plan, all right. You told them the secret word and everything, huh?

**Big Bird:** Yep. And when they hear it, they'll come running.

**Snuffy:** Oh, I hope I can be there to see that.

**Big Bird:** You *will* be. That's the whole idea.

**Snuffy:** Oh *yeah*, right.

*(And it seemed as if it was that simple—so simple that Snuffy decided that he wanted to go home and tell his mommy about the plan. Big Bird, seeing that Snuffy is about to leave, yells the secret word, "Food," and Bob, Linda, Maria, Luis, Susan,*

*Everybody's a lot closer to the ground than I am.—Snuffy*

**BORN:** August 19 (Leo)
Snuffy, like Bert, is a Leo—but Snuffy is born near the cusp, and is thus a little more mellow and proud (and less uptight) than Bert. He shares his sign with Bill Clinton (who once had a senior advisor named George Stephanopoulos), Lucille Ball ("Vitameatavegemin" is almost as hard to say as Snuffleupagus), and John Stamos (let's face it—Snuffy's a teen idol at heart).
**VOICE AND PUPPETRY:** Jerry Nelson; Martin P. Robinson
**FULL NAME:** Aloysius Snuffleupagus
**ORIGINALLY FROM:** Hawaii
**SCIENTIFIC NAME:** Snuffle upagus
**SHOE SIZE:** 65 GGG
**QUOTE:** "Oh, dear." (Try saying it slowly, holding your nose.)
**PHILOSOPHY:** Take it slow—real slow.
**FAVORITE SONGS:** "He Ain't Heavy"; "Something's Coming"
**BEST FRIEND:** Big Bird (he calls him "Bird")
**LIKES:** Games; cabbage; spaghetti
**DISLIKES:** When nobody believes he exists
**HOBBIES:** Roller-skating with Bird

40

Gordon, David, and a few others run out. But Snuffy is gone when the adults arrive. Big Bird is noticeably upset.)

**Bob:** Where *is* he, Big Bird?

**Big Bird:** Gone! Before I had a chance to yell "Food" he went home to tell his mommy what a great plan I had. Some great plan.

*(Linda assures him in sign language that it was a good plan.)*

**Big Bird:** If it's so good, how come it didn't work?

**Bob:** *(Softly)* Could it possibly be because Mr. Snuffleupagus is imaginary?

**Big Bird/Maria/Luis/Linda/Gordon** *(who have already been convinced that Snuffy's real)*: NO!

**Bob:** Just asking.

*(The adults convince Big Bird that what he needs is someone to help him keep Snuffy around after he yells "Food." Elmo pops up to help, and the adults leave. Big Bird and Elmo amend the plan slightly. When Big Bird yells the secret word, Elmo will hold onto Snuffy's snuffle so that he can't get away. Finally Snuffy returns. Big Bird yells the secret word once more.)*

**Big Bird:** Food! Food!

**Snuffy:** That means Bird's friends are going to come and meet me now!

**Elmo:** Yes! Now!

**Snuffy:** Oh, boy! I better go home and brush my fur. I want to look good for them.

**Elmo:** *(Holding Snuffy's snuffle tightly)* No! Can't go!

**Snuffy:** Yes, I have to go. Now let go of my snuffle!

*(A tug-of-war ensues between the small red monster and the furry pachyderm—Elmo struggles with Snuffy as the adults rush into the nest area. The tug-of-war takes them through the doors, and one by one, the adults go through the doors to see Snuffy. Big Bird is about to join them, but has last-minute second thoughts.)*

**Big Bird:** What do you think? *(To camera)* Should I open this door and maybe see the grown-ups face to face with Snuffy—or not? I should? I shouldn't? Well, which is it? Should! Right! Of course! It's about time! Let's get this over with. *(He reaches for the door, but stops)* I don't know why, but I feel like I'm saying good-bye to an old friend.

*(Big Bird opens the door, and over his shoulder we see what he sees—the full cast standing with mouths agape, completely stunned looks on their face as they look upon Snuffy and Elmo struggling.)*

**Big Bird:** At last!

**Susan:** All that time and we didn't believe you. It must have been hard.

**Big Bird** *(Sadly)*: It was.

**Susan:** I'm really sorry, Big Bird.

**Bob:** From now on, we'll believe you when you tell us something.

**Big Bird:** Promise?

**All:** Promise!

**Snuffy:** Maybe we should get that in writing....

## WHY SNUFFY WAS OUTED

It was 1985, and the writers had just about run out of ways for Snuffy to be "just missed" by the *Sesame Street* adults. Moreover, researchers had become worried about the message this was sending to children—that they might not be believed by the adults around them if they told them something unusual. If you couldn't trust Big Bird, whom could you trust?

At that time, increasing numbers of stories about child molestation and abuse were being told in the media. The *Sesame Street* educators worried that if children saw that the grown-ups didn't believe what Big Bird said (even though it was true), they would be afraid to talk to adults about dramatic or disturbing things that happened to them—afraid that adults wouldn't believe them, either.

So the writers and researchers decided that it was time to have Snuffy "become real" and be seen by the adult cast.

After fifteen years of bad timing, in all his furry, massive splendor, Snuffy was finally acknowledged as real.

"Snuffy kind of embraces the world with his heart. He's got tunnel vision to a certain extent. He sees one thing at a time, and switches from one to another."

—Martin Robinson

**Pssst!!**

### secret snuffleupafact:

Mr. Snuffleupagus was originally played by Jerry Nelson, but the costume hurt Jerry's back so much that he had to give up the part to Martin Robinson, who has played Snuffy for more than eighteen years.

# Where Were You the Day Mr. Hooper Died?

In 1982, the *Sesame Street* family lost a patriarch. Will Lee, who had played Mr. Hooper for more than thirteen years, died from cancer. "We had many discussions," says Norman Stiles, the head writer at the time. "We could just have another actor come in and replace Mr. Hooper, or we could, as a tribute to Will, use the moment to help preschoolers deal with death."

And in typical *Sesame Street* style, they dealt with it. Rather than replace Will Lee with another actor in the same role, the *Sesame Street* team of creators and researchers decided to do what they thought Lee would have wanted them to do—to mirror real life, to talk to kids truthfully, and to tell them what it really means when someone dies.

The writers talked to experts in the field of loss and separation who told them what *not* to say: not to say Mr. Hooper went to the hospital and died (because kids would be frightened of the hospital), *not* to say Mr. Hooper went away on a trip.

In the end, *Sesame Street* spoke straight to our hearts. They told us the truth. He had died, and he wasn't coming back. The producers decided to air the program on Thanksgiving Day, 1983, so that parents would be home and be able to discuss the episode with their children afterward. The response to the show was overwhelmingly positive. For everyone who missed that day on *Sesame Street*, and for everyone who just wants to remember, here's one of *Sesame Street*'s saddest—and most poignant—moments.

*(Big Bird approaches the* Sesame Street *adults—Maria, David, Luis, Linda, Gordon, Susan, and Bob—with portraits he's drawn of each of them. He presents the portraits, and then shows everyone the portrait he's drawn of Mr. Hooper. Big Bird tells everyone that he wants to give the picture to Mr. Hooper. The adults look at each other in confusion.)*

**Big Bird:** Where is he?

**Maria:** Big Bird—don't you remember? We told you—Mr. Hooper *died*. He's dead.

**Big Bird:** Oh yeah, I remember. Well, I'll give it to him when he comes back.

**Susan:** *(Pause)* Big Bird, Mr. Hooper's not *coming* back.

**Big Bird:** Why not?

**Susan:** Big Bird, when people die, they don't come back.

**Big Bird:** *(Sadly)* Never?

**Susan:** No, never.

**Big Bird:** *(With even more sadness)* Why not?

**Luis:** Well, Big Bird, they're *dead*—they can't come back.

**Big Bird:** *(Worried)* Well, he's *gotta* come back! Who's gonna take care of the store? And who's gonna make my birdseed milkshakes and tell me stories? *(Near tears)*

**David:** I'm gonna take care of the store. Mr. Hooper—he left it to me. And I'll make you your milkshakes—and we'll all tell you stories. We'll make sure you're okay.

**Big Bird:** *(Very sad)* Well, it won't be the same.

**Bob:** You're right, Big Bird. It'll never be the same around here without him. But you know something, we can all be very happy that we had a chance to be with him, and to know him, and to love him a lot when he was here.

**Olivia:** And Big Bird, we still have our memories of him.

**Big Bird:** Yeah. Yeah, our memories, right. Why, memories—that's how I drew this picture, from memory. Yeah. And we can remember him, and remember him, and remember him—as much as we want to. But I don't *like* it. It makes me sad. *(Cries)*

**David:** We all feel sad, Big Bird.

**Big Bird:** *(Sniffle)* He's never coming back?

**David:** Never.

**Big Bird:** Well, I don't understand. You know, everything was just fine. Why does it have to be this way? Give me one good reason.

**Gordon:** Big Bird, it has to be this way—*because*.

**Big Bird:** Just because?

**Gordon:** Just because.

**Big Bird:** Hmmm. You know, I'm gonna miss you, Mr. Looper.

**Maria:** *(Crying)* That's Hooper, Big Bird, Hooper!

**Big Bird:** Right.

*(They all gather around Big Bird for a hug.)*

## MR. HOOPER: THE MENTOR

Whatever little bit of acting I learned was pretty much all due to Will Lee. He was a great teacher.... I could hardly go near Hooper's Store for about a year after he died.

—Bob McGrath

The point is: Be honest. We could have really skipped it. He could have moved to Florida, he could have just disappeared with no explanation. We were brave.

—Loretta Long

I remember the last day I saw him. I thought, he is very ill, but he isn't talking about it. And so I put my arm around his shoulder–I had the bird feet on–and I said, "I love you Mr. Looper." And he said, "And I love you, Caroll." And that was our good-bye. He died four days later.

—Caroll Spinney

**Psssst!!**

secret fact:

The portrait Big Bird wanted to present to Mr. Hooper was actually drawn by Caroll Spinney, who is also an accomplished cartoonist. The portrait now hangs on the wall by Big Bird's nest. And in case you're wondering, no, Big Bird will never sell it, not ever—not even if you offered him a hundred bags of birdseed.

*1, 2, 3, 4, 5, 6, 7, 8, 9, 10.*
*Let's sing a song of 10!*
*How many is 10?*

**10** Toes!

**10** Pins!

**10** Toys!

Baker *(Jim Henson's voice):*

"Ten . . . Layer . . . Cakes!"
*(Trips, bumps, and*
*stumbles down the stairs,*
*dropping everything)*

**And that's**
**the song of 10!**

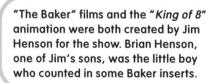

"The Baker" films and the "*King of 8*"
animation were both created by Jim
Henson for the show. Brian Henson,
one of Jim's sons, was the little boy
who counted in some Baker inserts.

# the ladybug picnic

1, 2, 3
4, 5, 6
7, 8, 9
10, 11, 12
Ladybugs came
To the Ladybug Picnic

1, 2, 3
4, 5, 6
7, 8, 9
10, 11, 12
And they all played games
At the Ladybug Picnic

They had 12 sacks so they
ran sack races
And they fell on their
backs and they fell on
their faces
Ladybugs 12
At the Ladybug Picnic

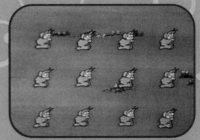

They played jump rope but
the rope it broke
So they just sat around
telling knock-knock jokes
Ladybugs 12
At the Ladybug Picnic

1, 2, 3
4, 5, 6
7, 8, 9
10, 11, 12
And they chatted away
At the Ladybug Picnic

They talked about the
high price of furniture
and rugs
And fire insurance
for ladybugs
Ladybugs 12
At the Ladybug Picnic
12!

# the nearness
## (and farness)
### of
# Grov

**I don't know how Grover came about. He just arrived.**
—Frank Oz

And he crash-landed, no doubt.

Grover is the Muppet we'd all like to be—self-confident, furry, cute, capable, and intelligent. Well, self-confident, furry, and cute, at least. He is committed, too, and we remember him not only as an adorable little monster, but also as the valiant teacher of *Sesame Street*, struggling to explain concepts no matter how difficult the odds. Concepts like: "Near" and "Far"; "Upstairs" and "Downstairs"; "Here" and "There"; and "Heavy" and "Light," to name just a few.

Grover always gets his message across, but not without great effort and a little suffering (not to mention a fainting spell or two). He is a teacher, a waiter, a professor, a farmer, an elevator operator, a salesman, and a supermonster. In fact, one could also argue that Grover represents *everymonster* as he constantly struggles to find his way in the world by helping those who need it. All this while remaining cute and adorable, too!

Here's a look at how he does it: Grover's Greatest Bits.

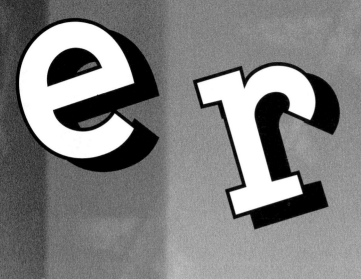

er

**Did You Know?** Grover is written to represent the psychological age of a four-year-old.

## HOW TO REMEMBER DIFFICULT ORDERS, ACCORDING TO GROVER THE WAITER

Grover is the consummate professional waiter. He does not need to *write* things down. He simply uses his "waiter's memory." When trying to remember orders, he makes up a little poem. For example, when his customer orders a cheeseburger with pickles and French fries:

*"Round and tasty on a bun*
*Pickles, French fries*
*Yum yum yum!"*

He uses the same technique to remember who gets what. For example, when his customer, coincidentally, happens to be a fat, blue, bald man:

*"In a hur-ry to be fed*
*Bea-dy eyes and big blue head!"*

## a LPHABET SOUP

Remember Grover the waiter? He worked at Charlie's Restaurant and never seemed to be able to satisfy his customer, Fat Blue. What follows is the first Grover the waiter sketch ever—and it's yet another clever way *Sesame Street* taught the alphabet.

*(Fat Blue is sitting at a table in a restaurant. Grover enters through the double doors from the kitchen)*

**Fat Blue:** Waiter!

**Grover:** *(Coming over to the table with a flourish)* Yes sir, hel-lo there! I am Grover, I am your waiter, and I am here to serve you. What can I get you, *hmmm*?

**Fat Blue:** Yes, I'd like a bowl of hot alphabet soup. And make sure it's *hot*.

**Grover:** Make sure it's hot. Okay, sir, coming right up. *(Rushing back through the double doors and shouting)* Hey Charlie, table 26 wants a bowl of hot alphabet soup!

**Fat Blue:** *(Sings alphabet)* A, B, C, D, E, F, G—

**Grover:** *(Returning through double doors)* Oh how hot this is! You are going to love this! Oh, look at that *delicious* soup.

**Fat Blue:** I'll just check this out.

**Grover:** Check what out?

**Fat Blue:** The soup.

**Grover:** *Bon appetit*, sir. *(Leaves)*

**Fat Blue:** *(Speaking)* A, B, C, D, E, F, G, H, I—*waiter*!

**Grover:** Yes sir!

**Fat Blue:** There's a J missing in this soup! I don't want it without a J.

**Grover:** J missing in the soup? Okay, I will get you the J. *(Heads back to kitchen through double doors*

*shouting)* Uh, Charlie, I think there is a J missing in the soup! *(Returns momentarily)* Okay, here is the J, sir.

**Fat Blue:** Well, put it in the soup!

**Grover:** *(Plop)* Okay, have fun.

**Fat Blue:** *(Saying the letters again)* A, B, C, D, E, F, G, H, I, J, K, L, M, N—*waiter*! *(Grover arrives)* Now the O is missing! I don't want this soup without an O!

**Grover:** It is a bad day for you, is it not, sir? Okay, I will get you the O—I will be right back. *(Heads back to kitchen again)* Charlie, I got a weirdo! This is silly. *(Returns momentarily)* Uh, sir? Sir, I have an O here for you. *(Plops it in the soup)*

**Fat Blue:** *(Saying the letters again)* A, B, C, D, E, F, G, H, I, J, K, L, M, N, O, P, Q, R, S, T, U, V, W, X, Y—

**Grover:** Do not tell me. Do *not* tell me—

**Fat Blue:** No good. The Z is missing!

**Grover:** All right, all right, do not rub it in! This is a good restaurant—I will get the Z! *(Leaves and returns)* Okay, sir, I think I am going to make you very happy now, I have the Z here. *(Plops it in the soup)*

**Fat Blue:** Okay, now let's see. *(Saying the letters again)* A, B, C, D, E, F, G, H, I, J, K, L, M, N, O, P, Q, R, S, T, U, V, W, X, Y and Z.

**Grover:** Okay! Now, I bet you are all happy.

**Fat Blue:** No—the soup's cold. Take it back and get me another bowl. *(Grover faints from exhaustion)*

**Z** Has sponsored show more than: 150 times
Has stood for: Zebra, Zip, Zoo

## WHAT GROVER HAS TAUGHT US

**Heavy and Light—** "This is a barbell. I will show you how heavy it is *(tries to lift it)*. Once more *(tries again)*. Oh, it is heavier than I thought *(falls backward)*. Well, I think that is enough about heavy today. Let us now talk about light, all right?"

**Here and There—** "Anywhere I am is HERE. Anywhere I am not is THERE."

**In and Out—** *(demonstrated in an elevator)* "Everybody IN. Is everybody IN? That is IN! Everybody OUT. Is everybody out? That is OUT!"

**BORN:** October 14 (Libra)
Grover's the typical Libra, working frantically one moment, and relaxing the next (never mind the fact that he's exhausted himself and collapsed on the floor). He shares his birthday with Roger Moore (unlike James Bond, however, Supergrover never gets the girl), Ralph Lauren (who may be chic, but isn't as cute as Grover), and Mahatma Gandhi (can't you see him doing "Near" and "Far"?).
**VOICE AND PUPPETRY:** Frank Oz
**SCIENTIFIC NAME:** Cutius bluicus
**QUOTE:** "Hello every-bod-eeeee!"
**PHILOSOPHY:** Always try to help others.
**FAVORITE SONGS:** "Monster in the Mirror"; "I Will Survive"
**BEST FRIEND:** Kermit (no one else has the patience)
**LIKES:** Righting wrongs (or thinking he is); anything served at Charlie's Restaurant; soaring high in the air as Supergrover; running upstairs and downstairs; wearing his Supergrover costume
**DISLIKES:** Phone booths without doors (supermonsters need their privacy, too!)
**HOBBIES:** Saving the day

> I think I will take a little nap. Right here.
> —Grover

Grover wants to help, and he tries his very hardest. Even in his language—he does not use contractions like CAN'T or WON'T. He's soft, and he's loyal, and he's cute, but at the same time if you push him too far he gets very upset and won't take any guff.
—Frank Oz

## NEAR AND FAR

Valiant as always, adorable, furry old Grover was always the one who would teach us about a new concept—or swoon from exhaustion while trying. Opposites were his nemesis, but Grover made sure that we always understood the contrasts, often at his own expense.

I, little, furry Grover, am going to show you "Near" and "Far."

THIS IS *NEAR.*

*(runs way back)*

This is *faaaaaar*!

*(runs up to the front again)*

THIS IS

You see? Oh. Okay, I'll do it once more for you. Okay? Okay!

*NEAR.*

THIS IS *NEAR.*

*(runs way back)*

This is *faaaaaar*!

**ssst!!** **secret fact:** Grover once performed this skit on *The Tonight Show* with Johnny Carson soon after *Sesame Street* became a hit.

*(runs back to the front again, panting)*

THIS IS *NEAR!*

*(runs way back,*

*completely exhausted now)*

This is- *(he faints)*

SMARTER THAN A SPEEDING BULLET

FURRIER THAN A POWERFUL LOCOMOTIVE

ABLE TO LEAP TALL SANDWICHES IN A SINGLE BOUND!!!

LOOK... UP IN THE SKY!

IT'S AN EGGPLANT!

IT'S A MEATBALL!

IT'S...

**SUPERGROVER!**

**We superheroes bruise easily, you know.**

—Supergrover

## SUPERGROVER'S RULES OF SUPERMONSTERDOM

Being a supermonster is not all glamour and gratitude, you know—it is a lot of work! In fact, it can be quite dangerous. So for all those out there who might *think* they are cut out to be a supermonster but are not sure, here are a few key rules to remember.

- ✿ **If at first you do not succeed—give up.**
- ✿ **Learn to crash-land with flair.**
- ✿ **Fighting is never the solution—a supermonster could get hurt!**
- ✿ **If you cannot fly away, look down. You may be step-ping on your cape. If that does not work, try, "Wubba wubba wubba." It may not help, but it could not hurt.**
- ✿ **Always remember to open the door before you fly away.**

## FURTHER ADVENTURES OF SUPERGROVER

Little Judy Finstermacher's grocery bag has broken and she doesn't know how she's going to get her groceries home. High above, Supergrover hears her cry for help:

**Supergrover:** AAAAAAAAAARRRRRRRGGGGGGHHHHHHH! *(crashes)*

**Little Girl:** Everything okay?

**Grover:** Yes—except for this super headache. *(Sees her groceries all over the ground)* Are you having a picnic?

*(The little girl explains that her bag broke and that she doesn't know how she's going to get all her groceries home.)*

**Grover:** Ohhhh, do not cry little girl.

**Little Girl:** *(Annoyed)* I wasn't planning to.

**Grover:** Oh. My superbrain will find a way to cope.

*(Supergrover remembers that he has a Supergrover Emergency Kit that might be of assis-*

**LOOK! Up in the sky**

I hit the floor so hard even my cape hurts.

*tance. He brings out a large box and offers her: Roller skates—to roll her groceries home, but this doesn't work.*

*String—to tie all the groceries together, but the little girl protests.)*

**Little Girl:** I don't think string would work very well.

**Grover:** I did not say, "*Very well,*" I just thought....

*(Grover continues to dig, and comes up with:*

*Glue—to glue the groceries together "in a big globule," but this doesn't work.*

*A tambourine—just because it's in there, but this also doesn't work.)*

**Grover:** Okay, you know, super ideas do not grow on trees!

*(Eventually, the little girl figures out for herself that she can use the box the Emergency Kit came in to tote her groceries home. Grover, of course, bursts with pride at having saved the day.)*

**Grover:** Ah! Supergrover has done it again. Yes! Protector of small chil-dren and bunny rabbits! A monster of extreme cuteness, doing brave deeds around the world.

*(The little girl goes home—but now Supergrover has no way to carry his Emergency supplies. There is only one thing to do—he hails a cab.)*

## SUPERGROVER, COMPUTER REPAIRMAN

A little girl cannot get her computer to start, and Supergrover arrives *(loudly)* on the scene. He suggests that they hop up and down and say "Wubba wubba!" to fix it. While Grover is doing just that *(he so loves saying "Wubba wubba!")*, the little girl fixes the computer by turning it on. Supergrover once again takes credit for having saved the day.

## THE BARBER OF *SESAME STREET*

Trouble is brewing in the barbershop. A little boy is afraid that getting his haircut will hurt. Supergrover arrives to fix matters by explaining to the boy about life. "Hurt? Hurt? Of course it will hurt! But you must be brave, you must smile through your tears! You must endure the agony, bear the pain! Ignore the ouchness!" This does not help, but the barber steps in and shows the little boy and Supergrover *(and the viewer)* by example that haircuts don't hurt after all. "Well, it looks like Supergrover, noble hero of heroes, has done it again! I have made a great discovery! Haircuts do not hurt! No! And I must spread the word throughout the land! Haircuts do not hurt!"

## DIAL S FOR SUPERGROVER

A little girl is sad because she has homework to do, but she has promised her friend Bobby that she will come over. She doesn't know what to do—he'll be so disappointed. Supergrover, as always, has the answer. "Do not *tell* him! No news is good news!" The little girl points out that her friend will be waiting for her all day. So Supergrover has another idea—he will call to Bobby out the window. While Grover is busy shouting, the little girl remembers that she can use the telephone to contact her friend.

Supergrover finishes shouting and returns to the girl, who informs him that she has just spoken to Bobby on the phone. "Aha! So he *did* hear my supervoice and he telephoned you! No need to thank me little girl, it is just another job well done by—*Supergrover*!"

### SUPERGROVER'S MODEST THANKS:

✿ Do not try to thank me—I live to serve.

✿ Do not thank me! It is my job.

✿ Oh, please do not thank me! Helping people is my joy and pleasure.

# What We Learned On *Sesame Street*

Here's a small sampling of subjects kids have learned about on *Sesame Street* over the years, excerpted from the *Sesame Street Curriculum Overview—29th Experimental Season of Sesame Street Statement of Instructional Goals*. This research document, written at the beginning of each season (this list is from the twenty-ninth), points to the show's curriculum goals for the year and summarizes the goals of past years.

Imagining
Inclusion
Japanese Americans
Korean Americans
Land forms
*Silence is golden. —Slimey the Worm*
Latino Americans
Listening
Love
Marriage

Problem solving
Race relations
Reading
Recycling
Rejection
Remembering
Rhythm
Safety
School

*If you don't have anything nice to say—by all means, say it! —Oscar*

Acceptance
Addition
*No matter what happens, remain calm. And go for the sound bite. —Kermit the Frog*
Adoption
African Americans
Air
*Follow your dreams. —Prairie Dawn*
Asking questions
Birth
Body parts and
*Count your chickens before they're hatched—count them whenever you can. —The Count*
functions
Career awareness
Chinese Americans
Classification
Clues
Computers
*There is joy in everything. —Elmo*
Conflict resolution
Cooperation
Counting (up to 40)
Creativity
Cultural diversity

Differences and
similarities
Discrimination
Drawing
Ecology
Emergencies
Ethnic diversity
Exercise
Failure
Feelings
Filipino Americans
Following directions
Friendship
Geography
Handicaps
Hawaii
History
Hospitals
Hygiene

Measurement
(the) Mind
Music
Native Americans
New Mexico
New York City
Numbers
Nutrition
Peer pressure
Practicing and
planning
*The early bird catches the word—of the day. —Big Bird*
Pregnancy
Pride

Self-esteem
Senses
Shapes
Sharing
Sign language
Sorting
Spanish
Subtraction
Tolerance
Trial and error
Water forms
Women's roles
Writing

## ALL I EVER REALLY NEEDED TO KNOW I LEARNED ON *SESAME STREET*

Curriculum goals weren't the only things kids learned on *Sesame Street*. At the same time kids were learning about letters and numbers and sorting and relationships, there were many subtle but significant messages coming across as well. Messages about love, about life, about family and about friendship.

# "A-la-peanut-butter-sandwiches"

## The Amazing Mumford's magic words don't usually work the

way he wants them to. For example, once he wanted to conjure a rabbit out of his hat—but he turned Grover, his assistant, into a rabbit instead.

## "Shishkabob-bob-shazam!"

The Genie of the Toothpaste's magic words that conjure up Cookie's Three Wishes

"Hubbledy-bubbledy flippery fluff!
Magic fire, do your stuff!"

"Higgledy-piggledy ding dong dell!
Kettle of water, dig my spell!"

"Bumbledy-grumbledy diddley duck!
Magic chicken, bring me luck!"

The spells of the three Anything Muppet witches who were trying to conjure up something good to eat. They eventually make chicken soup by cooperating.

# ONE, ONE WONDERFUL COUNT

## HOW DO WE LOVE THIS NUMERICAL VAMPIRE? LET US COUNT THE WAYS.

**One:** He's mysterious. What is it that drives him to count so obsessively? Where does he come from? (Transylvania—that's easy.) Does he come from a good, royal family? What color is his blood? And if he's a vampire, is he actually the undead, or simply the unnumbered? His mystique is undeniable.

**Two:** He's a romantic. No other Muppet is as passionate as The Count. As obsessive, maybe. But not as romantic. It's no accident that he has two girlfriends (two vonderful girlfriends, ah-ah-ah!—Countess Von Backwards and Countess Dahling von Dahling). Let's face it—he's a playboy.

**Three:** He's got the weather on his side. You know you were always waiting for that final number so you could hear the crack of thunder, see the flash of lightning—and to hear his trademark sinister laugh!

**Four:** He's a total clotheshorse. The turned-up collar, the monacle—he's the epitome of classic style. And he was making capes *couture* before *Batman* was a twinkle in George Clooney's, Val Kilmer's, or even Michael Keaton's eye.

**Five:** Let's face it, The Count knows what *counts*. No matter where he is, whether he's at home in his castle, talking with his friends on the street, hobnobbing with celebrities, or simply exploring the world around him, The Count can always find something to count.

### SAT: SESAME ACHIEVEMENT TEST (COUNTING SECTION)

**WHEN THE COUNT FINISHES COUNTING, THUNDER SOUNDS AND LIGHTNING FLASHES. WHAT HAPPENS WHEN GRANDPA COUNT FINISHES COUNTING?**

A  ○ He coughs
B  ○ It rains
C  ○ It snows
D  ○ Numbers fall from the sky

*Answer: C. This weather thing runs in the family.*

### Did You Know?

Count von Count is written to represent an adult with the psychological age of someone who is 1,832, 652 years old—and still counting. Sort of refreshing that after all those years he still gets a thrill from counting, isn't it?

**BORN:** October 9 (Libra)
Like most Libras, The Count tries to maintain the perfect balance between sanity and obsession. Libras can be superficial, eccentric, frivolous, and flighty (it all adds up!). He shares his sign with Charlton Heston (he sure could count those Commandments), Ed Sullivan (who counted acts), and T.S. Eliot (who counted cats).

**VOICE AND PUPPETRY:** Jerry Nelson
**SCIENTIFIC NAME:** Countus obsessivus
**QUOTE:** "Greetings! I am The Count. They call me The Count because I love to count things."
**PHILOSOPHY:** Count your blessings. Over and over and over and over....
**FAVORITE SONGS:** "Born to Add"; "Count on Me"
**BEST FRIENDS:** Creepy, his bat, and Fatita, his cat.
**LIKES:** Black capes; widow's peaks; hair gel; high collars; thick accents; and the concept of infinity.
**DISLIKES:** The concept of zero; calculators
**HOBBIES/OBSESSION:** You guessed it—counting!

**secret fact:**

When Jon Stone, *Sesame Street* head writer and director, read Norman Stiles' first Count script, he sent it back with a note scribbled across the top: "Good character, bad bit." So Norman scrapped the bit, kept The Count, and he's been enumerating ever since.

# ONE, TWO, THREE— THREE LITTLE PIGS!

The Count infiltrates Kermit's already problematic fairy-tale world in this classic episode of *Sesame Street* News.

**Kermit:** Kermit the Frog, your man in the street reporter here, and today we are going to interview the occupants of this house right here— the three little pigs. *(Mysterious music—The Count appears)*

**Count:** Three? Three little pigs? Wonderful! I will count them as you talk to them.

**Kermit:** No, I don't think that would work.

**Count:** Nonsense! Counting always works. Proceed.

**Kermit:** Well— *(Goes to the door and knocks)*

**Count:** One! One knock!
**Kermit:** Right. One knock. *(Knocks again)*
**Count:** Two knocks!
**Kermit:** Will you stop that! *(A pig answers the door)*
**Pig #1:** Yes?
**Kermit:** Kermit the Frog here, of *Sesame Street News*—

**Count:** One! One pig!

**Pig #1:** Who's that?

**Kermit:** Don't pay any attention to him, ma'am. He's just—

**Pig #2:** *(Coming to door)* Who is it, Margaret?

**Kermit:** Kermit the Frog of *Sesame*—

**Count:** Two! Two pigs!

**Pig #2:** What's going on out here?

**Pig #1:** I don't know. This frog knocked on the door and then this other guy started counting.

**Kermit:** Kermit the Frog of *Sesame Street News*—

**Pig #3:** *(Coming to door)* What's all the ruckus out here?

**Count:** Three! Three little pigs, ah, ah, ah! *(Thunder and lightning)*

**Pig #1:** What was that?

**Pig #2:** Shut the door. I think it's going to rain.

**Pig #3:** Who were those two weirdos?

**Pig #1:** Some frog, I don't know... *(They slam the door)*

**Kermit:** Well, so much for the, uh, three little pigs. Thanks a lot, Count. Well, maybe we'll have better luck next door here. *(He walks to the door. The Count walks with him.)* Will you get lost!

**Count:** Pay no attention to The Count. I will be silent as a mouse.

**Kermit:** Good!

**Count:** Unless I find something to count. *(Sees a pussy willow)* One. One pussy willow. *(Kermit knocks on the door)* One! One knock!

**Kermit:** Stop with the counting! We're on television here!

**Count:** *(Looks at camera)* One camera. *(A dwarf answers the door)*

**Kermit:** Kermit the Frog of *Sesame Street News*—

**Count:** One! One little person!

**Kermit:** Pay no attention to him. It's the house of the seven dwarfs!

**Count:** I will count them.

**Kermit:** Thank you. *(Double take)* No! Then that means...*(Dwarfs suddenly appear at every window)*

**Count:** Oh, happiness! One! One dwarf! Two! Two dwarfs! Three! Three dwarfs! *(Enters house and continues counting)*

**Kermit:** How am I supposed to do a television program when you keep counting every...*(Comes close to lens, in an aside to camera)* Can't you get this guy out of here? Oh yeah? Well, the same to you, fella! *(Back to Count)* Listen, you. I've had just about enough of— oh, nuts. This is Kermit the Frog returning you to your local studios. *(He leaves)*

**Count:** Seven! Seven dwarfs, ah ah ah! *(Thunder and lightning)*

## MUTINY OF THE BATTY

*(The Count is sitting in his castle, looking dramatically out his window. Bats are circling over him angrily.)*

**Count:** *(Noticing the bats are angry)* What is wrong, my darlings? Why are you so angry?

**Creepy the Bat:** *(Flying forward)* We bats are getting mad. We want our rights! We're going on strike.

**Count:** Going on strike? But why, my pets?

*(Bats murmur as if holding a conference)*

**Creepy:** You've given us a fine home, but we never get to count!

**Bats:** *(Chanting)* It's our turn to count! It's our turn to count!

**Count:** Ah! I think I know what to do! My friends, my bats—you will get to count! You, my little darlings, will get to count all the counts in the room. And then I, The Count, will count all the bats. First you, my pets.

**Creepy:** Whaddya mean count all the counts? There's only one of you here!

**Count:** Precisely! One wonderful Count! Ah ah ah! *(Thunder and lightning)* Now it is my turn.

**Bats:** Hey! Wait a minute! What's that? One Count? What a ripoff!

**Count:** *(Ignoring them)* And now my lovelies, I am counting! One bat! Two bats! Three bats! Four bats! Five bats! Six bats! Seven! Seven bats! Seven wonderful bats! Ah ah ah! *(Thunder and lightning)*

> To an old-fashioned Transylvanian girl you do not just say, "I love you." First, you must woo her.
> —The Count

## FIFTY WAYS TO WOO YOUR LOVER, ACCORDING TO THE COUNT

Ah, if only love were as predictable and constant as numbers are. But alas, such is not the case. Even The Count himself has found this to be true. So he resorts to what we all resort to—pitching woo. Here is his technique for winning The Countess's favor.

1. Use your charm and romantic mystique to win her over. Employ a vast array of pet names, such as:

   ❧ My little wombat
   ❧ My little armadillo
   ❧ My little sorceress
   ❧ My little wood pigeon

2. Bring her gifts, such as:

   ❧ A dozen long-stemmed Romanian beauty roses (that you've counted yourself, of course)

   ❧ A box of chocolates (if she is anything like you, she will simply count them, and ignore you).

3. Eventually, you will discover that with a Countess, gifts are a dead end. As The Count says, "Give her anything and she will count it. Give her the measles and she will count them."

4. There's only one way to make her happy. Approach her slowly, and tell her that you have one more thing to give her. Give her a kiss. She will be overwhelmed with desire—to continue counting. Give her another kiss, and another, and another; as she counts each one, she will fall more in love with you as she counts higher and higher!

*pssst!!*

**secret fact:**
The Count and Mumford the Magician have the same head, but different eyes, noses, and hair.

## THE COUNT VS. COOKIE MONSTER

Well, it wasn't as big a hit as Godzilla vs. Megalon or even Rocky vs. Apollo, but the encounter (pun intended) between The Count and Cookie Monster was memorable, nonetheless. Two obsessions

collided with hilarious results—and a little lesson about COOPERATION.

**Count:** Greetings! I am The Count. They call me The Count because I love to count things!

**Cookie Monster:** *(Clearly impressed with The Count's intro, Cookie decides to give it a shot)* Hi. Me Cookie Monster. They call me that because me love to eat *cookies*!

*(They notice a pile of cookies on a nearby plate)*

**Both :** COOOOKIEEES!

**Cookie Monster:** Me will *eat* them!

**Count:** No, I will *count* them.

**Cookie Monster:** Eat!

**Count:** No, count!

**Cookie Monster:** Eat!

**Count:** Count!

**Cookie Monster:** No, *eat*!

**Count:** Wait—why don't we cooperate?

**Cookie Monster:** You mean...

**Count:** Yes! I will count the cookies, and you will eat them!

**Cookie Monster:** Count!

**Count:** My pleasure. One!

**Cookie:** *(Eats cookie)* Yum yum yum...

**Count:** Two!

**Cookie:** *(Eats cookie)* Yum yum yum...

**Count:** Three!

**Cookie:** *(Eats cookie, more voraciously)* Yum yum yum...

**Count:** Four!

**Cookie:** *(Eats cookie, getting more frenzied)* Yum yum yum...

**Count:** Five!

**Cookie:** *(Eats cookie faster and louder)* Yum yum yum...

**Count:** Six!

**Cookie:** *(Getting really worked up now)* Yum yum yum...

**Count:** Seven!

**Cookie:** *(Eats last cookie in a complete whirlwind)* Yum yum yum...

**Count:** Seven cookies, ah ah ah! *(Thunder and lightning—the Count dramatically exits)*

**Cookie:** Ohhhhh! Ohhhhh! Cookies! *(Exits dramatically as well)*

# The Alligator King

**A** Has sponsored show more than: 150 times
Has stood for:
Acorn, *Abierto*, *Agua*, Alligator, Ape, Astronaut

The first son brought 7 oyster pearls from the bottom of the China Sea.

The second son gave him 7 statues of girls with clocks where their stomachs should be.

The fifth son brought the king perfume in 7 fancy silver jars.
The King took a whiff and he broke out in spots 'cause it smelled like cheap cigars.

The sixth son gave him 7 diamond rings to wear upon his toes.
The King snagged his foot on the royal red rug and rumpled up his nose.

Said the Alligator King to his 7 sons,
"I'm feeling mighty down,
"Whichever of you can cheer me up will get
to wear my crown."

The third son gave him 7 rubies from the
Sheikdom of Downtherebeneath.
The King thought the rubies were cherries,
and he broke off 7 of his teeth.

The fourth son tried to cheer him up
with 7 lemon drops.
The King said, "I'm sorry, son, since that ruby
episode I just haven't got the chops."

The seventh son of the Alligator King was a
thoughtful little whelp.
He said, "Dad, it appears to me that you
could use a little help."
Said the Alligator King to his seventh son,
"My son, you win the crown."

"You didn't bring me diamonds or rubies, but
you helped me up when I was down.
"Take the crown, it's yours, my son.
"I hope you don't mind the dents.
"I got it on sale at a discount store—cost me
all of 7 cents!"

7!

COOKIE, COOKIE, COOKIE, COOKIE, COOKIE, COOKIE, COOKIE, COOKIE, COOKIE, COOKIE, COOKIE, COOKIE, COOKIE, COOKIE, COOKIE, COOKIE, COOKIE, COOKIE, COOKIE, COOKIE, COOKIE, COOKIE, COOKIE, COOKIE, COOKIE, COOKIE, COOKIE, COOKIE, COOKIE, COOKIE, COOKIE, COOKIE, COOKIE, COOKIE, COOKIE, COOKIE, COOKIE, COOKIE, COOKIE, COOKIE, COOKIE, COOKIE, COOKIE, COOKIE, COOKIE, COOKIE, COOKIE, COOKIE, COOKIE, COOKIE, COOKIE, COOKIE, COOKIE, COOKIE, COOKIE, COOKIE, COOKIE, COOKIE, COOKIE, COOKIE, COOKIE, COOKIE, COOKIE, COOKIE, COOKIE, COOKIE, COOKIE, COOKIE, COOKIE, COOKIE, COOKIE, COOKIE, COOKIE, COOKIE, COOKIE,

**BORN:** November 2 (Scorpio)
Cookie, like all Scorpios, knows what he wants, and constantly schemes to get it. He shares his sign (but not his cookies) with Roseanne, Vivian Leigh (an actress obsessed), and David Schwimmer (who eats all of his friends' cookies).
**VOICE AND PUPPETRY:** Frank Oz
**SCIENTIFIC NAME:** *Voracious appetiticus*
**QUOTE:** "Me want cookie!"
**PHILOSOPHY:** You can never have too much of a good thing!
**FAVORITE SONGS:** "C is for Cookie"; "Hungry Like the Wolf"; "American Pie"
**BEST FRIEND:** Ernie (he often stays over when Bert's out of town)
**LIKES:** The four food groups (and any others you can find); The Joys of Eating (favorite book); creative problem solving through munching
**DISLIKES:** Empty plates; eating the last cookie
**HOBBIES/OBSESSION:** Eating lunch, eating dinner, eating snacks, eating telephones, eating Ws, eating umbrellas, and of course, eating cookies.

At first glance, Cookie Monster appears to be a monster with a one-track mind. He is deeply, emotionally, physically, and spiritually attached to cookies. Any kind of cookies. Chocolate Chip. Ginger Snaps. Sugar. Fudge. You name it, he eats it.

But in reality, Cookie is a deeply complicated monster. He's philosophical—he understands when to ask questions and when to act. ("Ohhhh! Coo-kies! Where they come from?... Whoooo cares! Come to papa!")

He's always ready to help a friend and to relieve them of, oh, say, a few excess cookies. ("Me know what to do. Eat Coookieeees!")

He's a monster of economy. He can convey worlds of meaning with a simple gesture—a slump of his furry shoulders ("What???? No cookies? What me going to do?"), fingers drumming on a table ("Where cookies at? Why me have to wait so long for cookies?") or on his chin ("How me going to get *that* cookie?"), or a long, agonizing howl ("Ohhhhh, no more cookies!!!!").

He's also in touch with his inner child: when he's confronted with the horror of an empty cookie jar he immediately bursts into tears. And he's environmentally aware—he eats the plate when he's done with his meal.

But these days he's also health conscious—he now eats meats and fish and vegetables, in addition to a variety of other foods (and objects). He's a creative problem-solver, too—when things don't go as planned, he can always eke out (or eat out) a solution.

Yes, Cookie is clear about his needs. He knows what he wants. Frank Oz (the man behind Cookie) sums it up best: "It's his one obsessive thing... if he has cookies he's happy. And I think it would be wonderful if all of us had only one thing that we needed to be happy."

Here are some of his tastier moments.

## COOKIE'S THREE WISHES

Here is the classic fable about a monster and his intense desire for cookies—and the differences between "small," "bigger," and "biggest."

(Once upon a time, in a faraway kingdom, there lived a furry monster. And one day, as he was brushing his teeth, a strange thing happened. A poof of smoke came out of the toothpaste tube, and in the middle of the smoke stood a little man... )

**Cookie Monster:** Who you?

**Genie:** Me? Oh, I'm the Genie of the Toothpaste! I've been stuck inside that tube of toothpaste for three and a half weeks! You squeezed the tube and set me free! And I'm so glad to be out of there that I'll tell you what I'm gonna do. I'm gonna give you three wishes. Any three wishes you want, you just tell me, and I'll make them come true.

**Cookie Monster:** You—little man—give monster three wishes? Oh boy! Lemme see... what me wish for? Hmm... it not easy.

(Cookie Monster decides to wish for a million cookies—but he realizes that he'll need something to carry the cookies in.)

**Cookie Monster:** Me wish for—truck! You give me truck?

**Genie:** Will I ever!

Shishkabob-bob-shazam! (Poof of smoke—a toy truck appears) Hey, I did it! Look, there's a truck! I haven't lost my touch! Howd'ya like it?

(Cookie is not satisfied—the truck isn't big enough to hold a million cookies. After a brief discussion with Bob, Cookie knows just what to do.)

**Cookie:** Me wish for—bigger truck!

**Genie:** You want it, you got it! Shishkabob-bob-shazam! (Poof of smoke—a slightly larger toy truck appears)

Hey, get a load of that! That's a nifty truck! Howd'ya like it?

**Cookie Monster:** (Staring at truck and clearly not satisfied) Well, it okay... (Cookie realizes that if he's going to wish for a million cookies, he'll need something even bigger) Genie, me know what to wish for this time. Give me—biggest truck of all!

**Genie:** One big truck, coming up! Shishkabob-bob-shazam! (Poof of smoke—actual pick-up truck appears behind them)

**Cookie Monster:** (Staring at truck) Fantastic! That perfect!

Truck will easily hold million cookies! Okay, Genie, do your stuff! Now me ready for biggest wish of all! Me wish for—million cookies! Million cookies! Do it! Do your thing! Me stand back. Give you room. Gimme million cookies—go Genie!

**Genie:** Yes, well... you see, we've got a problem. You see, I can't grant your wish for cookies because you've already had your three wishes.

**Cookie Monster:** Me have?

**Genie:** Yeah, well, look. The three things you wished for are right here. The *small* truck is one, the *bigger* truck is two, and the *biggest* truck makes three.

**Cookie Monster:** Me good at eating, but me not so good at counting.

**Genie:** Well, I'm really sorry, but you got your three wishes.

**Cookie Monster:** (Thinking creatively) Wait! If me hungry and there no cookies, only one thing to do—eat truck! (And so, Cookie Monster, piece by piece, devours the truck. And ate happily ever after.)

### HOW COOKIE MONSTER GOT A VOICE

I remember going into Dave Connell's office and saying, "Is it okay if one of the monsters talks?" And he said, "Well, they haven't ever talked before, and they're scary." And I said, "Well, what if they talked very little and I try to make it funny?" He said, "Well, go ahead—but don't have them talk very much."

—Jeff Moss, former head writer for *Sesame Street*

So Jeff wrote a bit for a "googly-eyed monster" and Ernie, in which the "googly-eyed monster" comes in and tries to steal Ernie's milk and cookies—in fact, those were the only two words the monster says: "Milk" and "Cookies."

From then on, it was Cowabunga!

They're round and simple—they're pure. And there's a whole lot of different kinds of them. You never get tired of them.

—Frank Oz on why Cookie Monster loves cookies

*pssst!!*

**secret fact:**
Because chocolate, oil, and grease can damage a Muppet, propmakers rarely use actual cookies on the show. If they do, they use only fat-free oatmeal cookies. But more often, propmakers use rice cakes and paint them to look like the cookies du jour. Cookie Monster doesn't mind, of course. He'll eat anything.

Me love to look out the window at night. See all the pretty stars—twinkle, twinkle. You know what moon remind me of? It remind me of great, big, delicious cookie!

—Cookie Monster

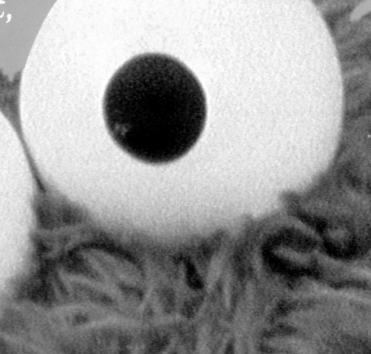

# Pip pip, and good evening. Alastair Cookie here. Me delighted to welcome you to Monsterpiece Theater.

—Cookie Monster as Alastair Cookie

## MONSTERPIECE THEATER

When it comes to classy drama, nothing classier than the extreme classiness of Monsterpiece Theater. It hosted for many years now by erudite—and very hungry—Alastair Cookie (was so hungry that in first few episodes ate own pipe at end of story).

In past, Monsterpiece Theater been place to see *Sesame Street* Muppets in wonderful and dramatic productions, like *Me, Claudius*, and of course, historic musical, *The King and I*.

And now, me proud to present collection of best pithy intros from Monsterpiece Theater.

Today, me incredibly proud to present one of best-loved classics in whole world. A play that explores feelings that bubble deep inside all of us. Yes, me proud to present *Hamlet, Prince of Denmark*. It not get classier than this.

Tonight, me present good old fashioned musical called *Guys and Dolls*. It all about guys and their dolls.

Tonight, me proud to present blockbuster epic, *Dances with Wolves*. Lots of action, lots of excitement, lotsa buffalos!

Tonight, me very excited to bring you all time favorite movie—*Gone With the Wind*. Me not seen it yet, but me hear it about—the wind.

Tonight, me happy to bring you classic thriller. Suspenseful film called *The 39 Stairs*. Made by guy named Alfred.

Tonight, on Monsterpiece Theater—*Room at the Top*. Exciting story of young monster who starts at the bottom, but work hard to make it to the top.

Tonight another episode in mystery about a monster trying to guess a town's secret. A town called, *Twin Beaks*. A darn fine town.

Tonight me proud to present famous Broadway musical about life among peasants in Russia—lots a good singing, dancing—fiddle playing! Here it is—*Fiddler on the Roof!*

Tonight, me bring you classic musical called *The King and I*. It about a king and the letter I—that where they get the title from. Very good title.

Tonight, Monsterpiece Theater proud to present classic play, *The Taming of the Shoe*, by William Shoespeare, famous podiatrist. Trust me.

Ah, the *Sesame Street* parodies—that fine mix of takeoff, pop culture, and curriculum that has brought us so many wonderful sketches. The writers of the show have mastered this humorous genre over the past thirty years, in hundreds of hilarious (and educational) moments based on popular songs, books, films, and musicals. We know the obvious ones—*Monsterpiece Theater, Dial S for Snuffleupagus*—but here are a few you may or may not recall.

*A Fish Called Elmo*
*All the President's Cookies*
*And the Baa Goes on*
*As the Worm Turns*
*Sally Messy Yuckayel*
*Honey, I Shrunk the Snuffleupagus*
*M*A*T*H*
*Madame Bovine*
*Miami Mice*
*School, She Wrote*
*Seven Gifts for Seven Brothers*
*Some Like it Warm*
*Smellnose Place*
*The Ape of Wrath*
*The Search for the Holy Pail*

**MONSTERPIECE THEATER: PROGRAM GUIDE**

| | |
|---|---|
| **MONDAY:** | *Bye Bye Birdie* |
| | *Chariots of Fur* |
| **TUESDAY:** | *Cyranose de Bergerac* |
| **WEDNESDAY:** | *Dr. No* |
| **THURSDAY:** | *Me, Claudius* |
| **FRIDAY:** | *The Old Man and the C* |
| **SATURDAY:** | *Red Riding Cookie* |
| | *The Ticklish Patient* |
| **SUNDAY:** | *Upstairs/Downstairs* |
| | *Waiting for Elmo* |

## COOKIE ON THE IMPORTANCE OF THE WORD "IMPORTANT"

Hello. Today me here in local bakery to talk about a word—*Important*. When something is *important* it mean a whole lot to you. Look—see this oatmeal cookie? It *important*. It mean a whole lot to me. *(Eats cookie)* Yum yum yum.

Oh, see this chocolate-chip cookie? Chocolate-chip cookie mean a whole lot to me, too. *Important*! *(Eats cookie)* Yum yum yum.

But, me not want to make this butter cookie feel bad. It *important* too. *(Eats cookie)* Yum yum yum.

Oh, and this gingerbread cookie, very *important* too. *(Eats cookie)* Yum yum yum. Oh, in fact, all cookies very *important*. They mean a lot to me. They mean much more to my *tummy*! Cowabunga! *(Eats all remaining cookies)*

### SAT: SESAME ACHIEVEMENT TEST (MATH SECTION)

**THE NUMBER OF DIGITS ON BOTH OF COOKIE'S HANDS PLUS THE NUMBER OF DIGITS ON BOTH OF BIG BIRD'S EQUALS ___:**

A ○ 12
B ○ 14
C ○ 10
D ○ 16

*Answer: D. Cookie has ten fingers, and Big Bird has six.*

## do you remember?

❀ When Cookie Monster, dressed in rabbit ears, was "the cookie bunny"—the jolly blue rabbit who hippity-hops into town once a year—the guy who knocks himself out making beautiful colored cookies like these? He "hid" the cookies in his tummy, where no one was able to find them.

❀ When Cookie Monster convinced Ernie not to eat his cookies fast? He explained, "If you eat cookies fast, then they be gone in no time at all, and you have no more cookies to eat." He then shows Ernie how to eat cookies fast, then slow, then fast again, then slow again, until all of Ernie's cookies are gone.

❀ When Cookie Monster slept over at Ernie's and Bert's apartment, because Bert was out of town, and Cookie had bad dreams? He dreamt of cookies that he couldn't reach.

❀ When Cookie Monster helped to settle an argument between a boy and a girl who were fighting over a cookie by declaring that the smallest person would get the cookie—and then shrank himself down so that he was about ten inches tall?

### COOKIE MONSTER ON "FIRST" AND "LAST"

**Prairie Dawn:** Cookie Monster, which cookie are you going to eat first?

**Cookie:** Me think you have misconception about cookie-eating process. Me not worried about first. Me eat *all* cookies at same time.

**Prairie Dawn:** Which cookie are you going to eat last? *(Cookie can't decide, so Prairie picks for him)*

**Cookie:** Prairie, me sure you are right about all this educational stuff, but Prairie, but Prairie *(he's now hysterical)*, *but Prairie*—that the *last* cookie! If me eat that last cookie then no more cookies forever. Forever!

**Prairie Dawn:** Listen to me, Cookie. It is not the last cookie forever. It is just the last cookie for right now. There are lots of cookies in the world. There, there. *(Comforts him)*

**Cookie:** You sure? Okay! Cooooookieee! Come to Papa! *(Eats the last cookie)*

*Did You Know?*

Cookie Monster almost had a previous life in potato-chip commercials in the late 1960s. Jim Henson was hired by a potato-chip company to develop a little furry character with an obsession for potato chips. He invented the puppet, who was then called Arnold. But the Arnold commercials never made it to the small screen. The owner of the potato chip company didn't want the negative image of a monster—albeit a friendly monster—eating his chips.

—Cookie Monster snoring

UKULELE

PLAYS NICE.

TASTES NICE, TOO!
—Cookie on ukulele

U Has sponsored show more than: 120 times

Has stood for:

Up, Ukulele, Umbrella, Uniform

1, 2, 3, 4, 5, 6, 7, 8, 9
She's a real Martian beauty,
my number 9 cutie,
She has 9 hairs on her head.
1, 2, 3, 4, 5, 6, 7, 8, 9
Tied up in ribbons of red.

She has 9 little eyes, all the
same size
Lookin' up, down, 'round, and
straight ahead.
She has 9 little holes in her
turned-up nose
And she snores when she goes to bed.

She has 9 arms, that's one of
her charms,
Each just like the other.
Some people say she looks
like her dad,
Some say she looks like her mother.

She has 1, 2, 3, 4, 5, 6, 7, 8, 9
Little toes on her foot
She doesn't go shoppin' 'cause she
doesn't like hoppin'
So usually she just stays put!
9!

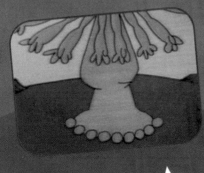

# A Brief Martian-English Dictionary

The *Sesame Street* Martians, in case you forgot, are those somewhat jellyfish-like creatures who speak in simple, declarative phrases that freely mix Martian and English. They scuttle about Earth, always looking for a new friend (in a telephone, a grandfather clock, a dripping faucet–whomever or whatever they happen to come across). Here's a Martian-English glossary, in case you ever run into one of them in your neighborhood.

**Yiiiiip–Yip Yip Yip Yip Yip!:** I think we're getting closer!

**Uh huh, Uh huh!:** I found it!

**Nope! Nope!:** Nope, I didn't find it.

**LookBook, LookBook:** Let's look in the book.

**Dung! Dung!:** I'm frightened–hide! (To do this effectively, place lower lip over your eyes and think you're hidden.)

**Drip drip, drip drip!:** What to say to a faucet that's trying to talk to you.

**BRRRRINGGG! BRRRRINGGG!:** What to say to a telephone that's trying to talk to you.

**BONNNNNG! BONNNNNG!:** What to say to a grandfather clock that's trying to talk to you.

BRRRRINGGG!

BRRRRINGGG!

# Prairie Dawn

**psssst!!**

## secret fact:

How Prairie Got Her Name

"I was sitting in an agent's office, trying to get representation, and there was a stack of 8x10 photos on the desk. I started to flip through them and I came across this actress—'Prairie Dorn.' I couldn't believe that someone had this name, 'Prairie.' So I came back to Jim Henson and said, 'I just came across this goofy name,' and then I don't know who came up with 'Dawn,' but obviously we didn't want to use this poor actress's name, 'Dorn,' so she became Prairie Dawn."

—Fran Brill, who performs Prairie Dawn

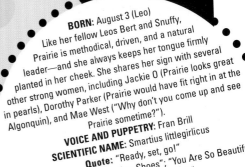

**Did You Know?**
Prairie Dawn is written to represent a little girl whose psychological age is that of a very precocious seven-year-old.

**Announcer:** And now it's time for science with *The Little Blonde Scientist Show.* And here she is the little blonde scientist herself.

**Prairie:** Hello. Today I would like to demonstrate to you how air moves things. I have placed on this table, as you can see, some leaves, a feather, and a brown paper lunch bag. Notice that the leaves, the feather, and the brown paper lunch bag are not moving. They are just lying here on this table. *(At this point Prairie politely yells up to the announcer)* Okay! Can you stir up a little wind please? Thank you. Although we cannot see it, smell it, or taste it, air is all around us,

and when air blows, it's called wind. And wind can move things. *(A huge gust of wind knocks everything off the table).* Oh my goodness! Oh dear! *(Screams to be heard above the gale)* See? Did you see how the wind blew everything away? Did you see how the wind blew away the leaves? And the feather? And the brown paper lunch bag? *(The wind is still blowing. Struggling to hold herself up against the gale force wind so that she doesn't blow away, Prairie is now screaming)* Ahhhhhhhhh! The place is going to blow away!

*(Prairie herself gets blown off the stage).*

**Announcer:** Tune in next time, fans for another episode of *The Little Blonde Scientist Show.*

*(Prairie stumbles back onto the stage with wild wind-blown hair, clearly exasperated and demands...)*

**Prairie:** All right. Who's working the wind machine?

## THE ORIGIN OF TELLY

Originally, Telly was Telly Monster, aka the "Television Monster." He was obsessed with watching television. His eyes had spirals in the center and were motorized so that they spun as he watched the tube. Ultimately, however, CTW producers felt that Telly might be perceived as a bad role model and were worried that kids would imitate him by watching television too close to the screen. So they changed Telly's spinning eyes to angst-ridden ones, replaced his TV monomania with a passion for triangles, and created the Telly viewers know and love today.

*Hope springs eternal in the heart of the American monster.*

—Martin Robinson on Telly

We know what you're thinking— "Who the heck is Telly Monster?" Telly is the hot (and cold—and hot) monster on the Street. He's one of the show's most popular Muppets today.

People think of Telly as the Woody Allen of Muppets: the neurotic one, the one who overthinks everything, the worrier.

"What if I can't do a good deed today?"

"What if I can't remember my promises?"

"What if I can't find a triangle?"

You get the drift.

Telly is passionate, particularly when it comes to helping others.

And about triangles. Telly loves triangles, every bit as much as Cookie loves cookies or The Count loves counting. So, of course, in Telly's case, that means he joins the Triangle Lover's Club and he publishes newsletters about the mysterious three-sided shape.

**BORN:** September 29 (Libra) Telly shares his sign with Grover and The Count, and like all Libras, he's up one minute and down the next. He is also always fully committed to whatever emotion he happens to be experiencing. He shares his sign with Charlie Brown (another great worrier), and Dr. Joyce Brothers (who certainly could help Telly resolve some of his issues).

**VOICE AND PUPPETRY:** Martin P. Robinson
**SCIENTIFIC NAME:** Verrius worrius
**QUOTE:** "Are you sure it's going to be all right?"
**PHILOSOPHY:** Don't be afraid to show your emotions—wherever and whenever possible.
**FAVORITE SONGS:** "Don't Cry Out Loud"; "Whistle a Happy Tune"; "Don't Worry, Be Happy"
**BEST FRIENDS:** Baby Bear and Oscar
**LIKES:** Counting to forty, being a member of the Bobketeers.
**DISLIKES:** Surprises; Woody Allen movies (too much anxiety); squares and circles.
**HOBBIES/OBSESSION:** Triangles, triangles, triangles!

To be or not to be? Telly is always thinking about what he'll be when he grows up. And everything sounds good, too—for a moment, at least.

A Firefighter—but it's a little dangerous.
A Chef—but being a cook is a messy job.
A Cowboy—but I don't want to fall off my horse.
A Construction Worker—but the noise might hurt my ears.

## HOW TO BE A BOBKETEER, ACCORDING TO TELLY

One day, Telly decided that Bob was his hero. (Didn't we all go through that phase at one point?) So he decided to become a "Bobketeer," to form a club that would follow Bob around and do everything he did. It didn't quite work out as Telly'd planned, but it was a good experience, nevertheless. Here are some ideas to get you started on forming your very own club!

## BOBKETEER CLUB RULES:

1.  Do everything Bob does. Knock on Bob's door before he wakes up. Bob will answer in his pajamas. Accidentally lock him out of his apartment. Get in Bob's bed and fall asleep until Bob's knocking wakes you. . . .

2.  Bob will want to shower. Since he won't let you shower with him, stand outside the bathroom listening and imitate what you think he's doing.

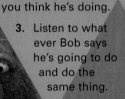

3.  Listen to whatever Bob says he's going to do and do the same thing.

4.  Get a few friends together and dress like Bob.

5.  Go for a jog with Bob and wear the same red sweatsuit.

6.  Get mad when Bob gets mad. Feel what Bob feels. For example, when he becomes furious after a bus passes him as he's standing at the bus stop, get angry with him. Say, "Come on, Bobketeers! Get angry!"

7.  When Bob wants to go to sleep, try to go to sleep with him. (He'll probably try to send you to your own home.)

8.  Suggest to him: "Let's do this again tomorrow." Bob will say, "Let's not." Ignore him.

### A TRIANGLE IS BORN

I remember I was home sick once, and I was watching my kid play with some triangles. I realized that I wanted to give Telly something that wasn't just neurotic, but a passion for something outside himself—and that became triangles.

—Lou Berger, *Sesame Street* head writer

## CLUBS YOU CAN JOIN ON *SESAME STREET*

It may not be the Hair Club for Men or the Psychic Friends Network, or even the Babysitters' Club, but *Sesame Street* has a selection of extracurricular activities all its own:

**The National Association of W Lovers**—President, Bert
Slogan: W—It's Like Getting Two Vs for the Price of One!

**The Triangle Lover's Club**—Local Chapter President, Telly
Slogan: Triangles—Not Just Your Average Shape! or With Three Sides, You're Bound to Like One of 'Em

**Club 40**—President, Telly; Officers, Elmo and Baby Bear
Slogan: 40—It's Bigger Than Ten, Twenty, Even Thirty!

**The Birdketeers**—President, Big Bird
Slogan: Be the Bird.

**The Grouchketeers**—President, Oscar
Slogan: Being a Grouch Isn't Just a Hobby—It's a Way of Life

**The Bobketeers**—President, Telly
Slogan: We're Just Looking for a Few Good Bobs

# Maria and Luis:
## The Course of True Love Gathers No Trash

**Oscar:** Yoo-hoo? Wake up there! What are you starin' at?

**Luis:** Oh. The way Maria walks.

**Oscar:** Well, what about it?

**Luis:** I don't know, it's kind of, uh, it's sort of, I guess a little special. It's funny I never noticed it before. *(Starts to walk away)*

**Oscar:** Oh! Hey, come back here! I think I see what you mean.

**Luis:** You see how Maria's walk is a little special?

**Oscar:** No, I was seeing how your walk is sorta special.

**Luis:** Mine? What's so special about it?

**Oscar:** Well, hard to say. Walk some more. *(Luis walks)* Aha! I got it! I know what it is about your walk that I like.

**Luis:** What?

**Oscar:** The way it takes you away from my trash can!

## PASS THE GUACAMOLE, PLEASE

Later that night, Maria invited Luis over for dinner. They made guacamole together. They were gushing about the guacamole, raving about the guacamole, and even kids could see it wasn't the guacamole that was so amazing.

Maria and Luis were just good friends for a long time. But in 1988, something changed. They started noticing each other more. They started looking at each other in a funny way. They started falling in love.

The Muppets couldn't figure out what was going on at first. Elmo heard Maria talking about Luis's wave and how cute it was, so Elmo decided to go check it out for himself. He asked Luis to wave for him, but couldn't see anything truly special there.

One day, Luis was talking with Oscar when Maria walked by. She said hello to them, and Luis stared at her as she walked away.

### *Ssst!!*
### secret fact:

It was a shotgun wedding! Sonia Manzano was already pregnant with Gabriela, her real-life daughter who ultimately played Gabriela on the show when the love/marriage sequence began. Her pregnancy gave producers the idea to deal with the course of love, marriage, and parenthood on *Sesame Street*. But they had to get her married off first. So when the wedding sequence was finally taped, the directors and producers had to design Maria's gown—and the camera angles—to hide the fact that she was pregnant with a future member of the cast. Ah, the magic of television....

## FIRST COMES LOVE, THEN COMES MARRIAGE, THEN COMES GABY IN THE BABY CARRIAGE

Eventually, Luis proposed, and a wedding date was set. It was to be the wedding of the century, ranking up there with the wedding of Diana and Charles, Joanie and Chachi, and Luke and Laura. All right, you get the idea. It was big.

All the residents of *Sesame Street* came to celebrate. It was a brief civil ceremony, but to viewers, it was bigger than the royal wedding.

The bride wore white, a stunning dress with a floral wreath on her head. The groom was dressed in formal black attire (no poofy shirt or light blue tux for our Luis!). Everyone on the Street was there: Big Bird, Bert and Ernie, Gina and David, Gordon and Susan, and many others, including Elmo (as the ringbearer) and Bob (who was best man).

The ceremony began, and the judge spoke. "We are gathered here today to celebrate the marriage of Maria and Luis. In front of you—the people they love most—their friends and their family..."

Luis and Maria both seemed to be swept up in the magic of the moment. At times, they seemed not to be hearing what the judge was saying. They gazed deeply into each other's eyes as if some plaintive love song was playing in their heads.

And then, after they were married, Maria became pregnant. It was as surprising for those on *Sesame Street* as it was for us—never before had a children's show explored the full course of love, marriage, and the making of a family. It was a moment that showed us the unpredictable magic of life. As Big Bird so aptly put it to Maria, "One minute you're fixing the toaster and the next there's a baby growing inside your body!"

When it was finally time for the baby to come, Oscar (believe it or not) was the one who helped Maria and Luis out the most (against his better judgment). When Maria went into labor, Gordon and Susan's car broke down. So it was Oscar who took Maria to the hospital in his sloppy jalopy.

*(Oscar and Luis at the hospital)*
**Oscar:** Luis, I've got a problem you need to help me with. Last night I drove you and Maria to the hospital and today I almost did you a favor by calling Hooper's. Now, why would I do a thing like that? I'm a Grouch! I'm not supposed to do nice things for people. But there's one more thing... it's important... I'm happy your baby is coming!
**Luis:** That's nice, Oscar.

**Oscar:** No—that's the problem. It *is* nice, and I'm a Grouch!
**Luis:** Oscar, relax. Babies make everybody happy. Deep down inside, you're still a Grouch. Just keep telling yourself, "I'm a Grouch, I'm a Grouch, I'm a Grouch."
**Oscar:** I gotta get home and get in my trash can—and I'm not coming out until I feel like my old self again.

*The baby eventually came, and Gabriela was welcomed into the Sesame Street family:*
**Marie:** Little baby, I want you to meet all our friends.
**Luis:** Friends, I want you to meet our little baby.
**Big Bird:** *(Tenderly)* It's nice to meet you, Gabriela. Welcome to *Sesame Street*— and the world!

# look ma, no script!

Some of *Sesame Street*'s most memorable moments occurred when children visited the Street. The kids would sit on that red brick wall and just talk about whatever came up. Whether they were counting or saying the alphabet together, discussing the meanings of different words, or just talking about life, these Muppet and kid moments are as genuine and as good as it gets. And what's amazing is that these moments were completely unscripted.

## GROVER AND JOHN-JOHN ON LOVE AND COUNTING

**Grover:** You know what, John-John?

**John-John:** What?

**Grover:** I love you.

**John-John:** *(Looks around for guidance—but realizes it ain't coming)* You love me?

**Grover:** Yes.

**John-John:** *(Looks around again)* Grover?

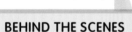

**Grover:** Yes?

**John-John:** You love me?

**Grover:** Yes—I love you, John-John.

**John-John:** Yeaaaah.

**Grover:** Yeah!

**John-John:** Yeah. *(Pause)* Count this penny.

**Grover:** Count that penny?

**John-John:** Yeah, count it.

**Grover** *(Looks at camera)*: Okay...

**John-John:** Count!

**Grover:** One!

**John-John:** One. *(Fade to black)*

## BEHIND THE SCENES

All the Muppeteers, directors, producers, writers, and anyone who's ever watched one of these moments being taped say the same thing—that the kids don't see the Muppeteers at all, even though they're sitting on the floor in plain sight. To the kids the Muppets are alive, the Muppeteers aren't even there.

Jane Henson, Jim Henson's wife and first Muppet partner, tells a story about a little boy who came to the set one day to tape a bit with Kermit. In between takes, the little boy stood with Jane and watched Jim rehearse with Kermit on his hand. Jane asked the little boy if he knew who the man was.

"Yep," said the little boy confidently. "He's the man who holds up Kermit while he's working."

## WHAT IS LOVE?

**Grover:** What is love?

**Chelsea:** Love is somethin' to do with hugs and kisses and a warm feeling inside.

**Grover:** Yeah! Boy. Love sounds great.

**Chelsea:** Mmm-hmm!

John-John was one of *Sesame Street*'s most memorable kid visitors. He made his debut on the show at the age of two back in 1971. Today, John-John is an accountant who lives in San Antonio.

## WHAT IS MARRIAGE?

**Grover:** Do you know what marriage is?

**Jesse:** Mm-hmm.

**Grover:** What is marriage?

**Jesse:** A marriage is when two people get married.

**Grover:** Yeah, that's good. That's marriage. What else is it when they get married— then what do they do when they're married?

**Jesse:** Kiss.

**Grover:** They kiss, yes. What else when they're married?

**Jesse:** Hug.

**Grover:** Hug, that's good. Anything else?

**Jesse:** Nope.

**Grover:** That's it?

**Jesse:** Yep.

**Grover:** Well, they live together—they help each other, don't they?

**Jesse:** Mmm-hmm.

**Grover:** 'Cause they see each other every day?

**Jesse:** Yep.

**Grover:** So it's important to help each other.

**Jesse:** Yeah, yeah, yeah.

**Grover:** Are they friends, also?

**Jesse:** Yep.

**Grover:** Well that's a lot in a marriage isn't it—kissing, hugging, friends, helping. All that stuff!

**Jesse:** Yep.

**Grover:** Well, I guess that's what marriage is about.

**Jesse:** Yep.

**Grover:** Thank you for your help.

**Jesse:** You're welcome.

## CAN YOU SING THE ALPHABET?

**Kermit:** Can you sing the alphabet, Joey?

**Joey:** Yes, yes, I could.

**Kermit:** Let's hear you sing the alphabet.

**Joey:** *(Letters appear above them as she sings)* A, B, C, D, E, F, G—Cookie Monster! *(Cookie Monster picture appears above them— she laughs at her joke)*

**Kermit:** *(Not amused)* You're not singing the alphabet! *(They sing together)* A, B, C, D, E, F, G, H, I, J, K, L, M, N, O, P, Q, R—

**Joey:** Cookie Monster!

**Kermit:** Cookie Monster isn't a letter of the alphabet. It goes, Q, R, S, T, U—

**Joey:** T, U—Cookie Monster!

**Kermit:** *(Scrunching his mouth)* You're just teasing me. W, X, Y, and Z. Now I've sung my A, B, Cs, next time—

**Joey:** *(Interrupting)* Cookie Monster!

**Kermit:** Next time Cookie Monster can do it with you. I'm leaving. Whew! *(Walks off)*

**Joey:** *(Hopefully)* I love you.

**Kermit:** *(Walking back)* I love you, too.

**Joey:** Oh! Thanks! *(Kisses his head)* Cookie Monster!

e

**Did You Know?**
Elmo is written to represent the psychological age of a three-and-a-half-year-old.

▼ TICKLE HIM, PLEASE

# I m O

Elmo with Ellen DeGeneres

Elmo with Whoopi Goldberg

Every so often you need some new blood to keep things lively.

Well, on *Sesame Street*, the attempt to mix things up brought us a little red dynamo named Elmo. CTW researchers wanted a toddler monster to join the Street—a monster who would have trouble keeping up with the older monsters and would help a younger audience identify with the show. Ergo, Elmo. He first appeared as a little red monster in 1979, but his identity and popularity surged when Muppeteer Kevin Clash started performing him in 1984.

We've all heard of Elmo by now—the Monster, the Myth, the Muppet of epic proportions. He's the Muppet that roared (well, giggled, anyway), the Cabbage Patch Kid of the 1990s—the monster who became the biggest selling toy in 1996.

Elmo with Linda Ronstadt

So who is this little red phenomenon, and what makes him tick? He's simplicity incarnate, but he's not simpleminded. Elmo's the eternal child ("Elmo loves to play!") and the perennial optimist ("Elmo loves you"). *Sesame Street* writers and Muppeteer Kevin Clash have somehow managed to distill the very essence of innocence and enthusiasm in Elmo. More than anything, Elmo always finds a way to show the good side of whatever situation he's in.

Meet the monster with the infectious laugh—the future of *Sesame Street* may be in his furry red hands.

**≈ssst!!**

## secret fact:

In 1996 and 1997, more than five million Tickle Me Elmos were sold, making it the hottest-selling toy in the world.

## BEAUTY IS FUR DEEP

*Whoopi Goldberg was on the show with Elmo in 1990. They shared the following moment, a moment that showed children how proud they should all be of who they are.*

**Elmo:** *(Strokes Whoopi's arm)* Wow! Elmo likes Whoopi's arm.

**Whoopi:** Thanks, Elmo.

**Elmo:** Elmo also likes this stuff that covers Whoopi's arm.

**Whoopi:** Oh, my skin?

**Elmo:** Yeah, skin! It's soft. And pretty, too. Elmo thinks Whoopi's skin is a very pretty brown.

**Whoopi:** Oh, well, thank you Elmo. You know what? I like your fur, too.

**Elmo:** Really?

**Whoopi:** It's a great color red. It's nice and bright. *(Touches him)* And soft, too. It's nice and—furry!

**Elmo:** Elmo's fur is furry all right. But it is not like Whoopi's skin. Yeah, Whoopi likes Elmo's fur and Elmo likes Whoopi's skin... Yeah, yeah. Let's trade!

**Whoopi:** No, no, we can't, Elmo. It's not possible. You can't trade things like hair and skin and fur. See? *(Pulls skin)* It doesn't come off. *(Grabs her hair)* My hair's on for good, too. It's just like your fur.

**Elmo:** *(Pulls his fur to see)* Ow! Yeah, Elmo see that.

**Whoopi:** But even if we could trade, Elmo, I wouldn't want to. I like my skin and my hair. And I'd like to keep them both. I mean, don't you like your fur?

**Elmo:** Well, yeah, Elmo likes his fur. And Elmo wants to keep his fur just where it is—on Elmo. Right next to Whoopi. *(They hug)*

**Whoopi:** I like that, too, Elmo.

**Elmo:** Yeah.

**BORN:** February 3 (Aquarius) Elmo, like Ernie, is an Aquarian—incurably friendly, curious, and full of surprise. He shares his sign with Mary Lou Retton (Tell me you wouldn't have bought a "Tickle Me Mary Lou" doll?), Jimmy Durante (their noses are similar), and Drew Barrymore (who was about Elmo's size when she starred in E.T.)
**VOICE AND PUPPETRY:** Kevin Clash
**SCIENTIFIC NAME:** Furrius childus
**QUOTE:** "That tickles."
**PHILOSOPHY:** Give love and you shall receive love.
**FAVORITE SONG:** "Elmo's Song"
**BEST FRIENDS:** Grover and Zoe
**LIKES:** Everything (You name it, he likes it); doing whatever Ernie and Bert can do
**DISLIKES:** Brussels sprouts (but who doesn't?)

# ELMO AS HAMLET, THE PRINCE OF LAUGHTER

Mel Gibson lent his Shakespearean flair to this *Monsterpiece Theater* segment he did with Elmo.

**Elmo:** Forsooth! Elmo spotteth Hamlet, Prince of Denmark. Reading a book. *(Mel laughs as he reads.)* A funny book! It maketh him happy! Oh Hamlet, what doth thou read that maketh thou so happy?

**Mel:** *(Happily)* Words, words, words.

**Elmo:** Elmo knoweth that a book hath words, words, words, but pray tell, what words doth the book hath? *(Mel begins to weep and doesn't answer.)* Oh, now Prince Hamlet seemeth so sad! Oh Hamlet, pray telleth Elmo what thou doth read that maketh thee so sad?

**Mel:** *(Sadly)* Words, words, words.

**Elmo:** Again with the words, words, words. Prince Hamlet doth not give gentle Elmo a straight answer. *(Mel doesn't answer—looks angry now.)* Uh-oh, uh-oh! A dark cloud doth sweep across Hamlet's brow! He seemeth angry! What doth thou read that maketh thee so angry, oh great prince?

**Mel:** *(Angrily)* Words! Words! Words!

**Elmo:** Okay! That does it! Elmo's feddeth up! *(Elmo leaves, then returns with a book. He sits down, opens it, and begins laughing.)*

**Mel:** What doth thou read, Elmo?

**Elmo:** Elmo can't read, Hamlet. Elmo's looking at pictures, pictures, pictures!

Elmo with Mel Gibson

**≈pssst!!**

secret fact:
Zoe was originally created to visually complement Elmo onscreen. For instance, the red in Zoe's mouth is the same color as Elmo's fur, and Elmo's nose is the same color as Zoe's fur.

**BORN:** September 30 (Libra) Simultaneously dainty and strong, practical and impulsive, Zoe shares her sign with Sharon Stone (and her basic instincts as well), Barbara Walters ("If you were a Muppet, which one would *you* be?"), and Nietzsche (the cute, furry philosopher?).

**VOICE AND PUPPETRY:** Fran Brill

**SCIENTIFIC NAME:** Teenius exciticus

**QUOTE:** "Don't joke me!"

**FAVORITE SONG:** "Let's Go Crazy"; "Put on a Happy Face"; "Jump"

**BEST FRIEND:** Elmo

**LIKES:** Mimi, her dolly; red monsters who giggle

**DISLIKES:** Sitting still and the training wheels on her bicycle

**HOBBIES:** Collecting necklaces, bracelets, and barrettes

**Zoe:** Hi, I'm Zoe and today I feel proud *(laughs)*. Do you know what proud is? Well, proud is when you feel really, really, really, really, really, really, really, really, really, really good about something you can do—like if you run around real fast *(Runs around in a circle)*. That makes you feel proud. Or, when you learn a new song *(Sings)* La-La-La-La-La. That makes you feel proud. Or, you know what I can do? I can fly a real plane *(Laughs)*. No, I'm too little. But, you know what I can do? *(Starts speaking in giberish)* Le-La-Bo-Be. That's what I can do and it makes me feel proud.

**Pssst!!**

**secret fact:**

When Michael Loman became the executive producer of *Sesame Street* in 1982, he wanted a young female monster as a main character on the show. So in 1993, Zoe came along. From several possible designs of the character, "I picked the one that had a face like Carol Channing," says Fran Brill. "I wanted her to be obviously female with jewelry and barrettes in her hair. Someone suggested that we call her Frannie, since that's my nickname. But I didn't want a Muppet with my name, so I thought of the J.D. Salinger book *Franny and Zooey*, and suggested Zoe, which seemed to be just right."

we interrupt
this broadcast
to bring you
a muppet
news flash

**BORN:** Leap Year Day (Pisces)
Like Big Bird, his fellow Piscean, Kermit is charming, good-natured, and not easily rattled. He shares his sign with Lou Reed (who sometimes has a frog in his throat), Michelangelo (who never painted frogs, but would have done a beautiful job), and Sally Jessy Raphael (a great interviewer in her own right).
**VOICE AND PUPPETRY:** Jim Henson (now played by Steve Whitmire)
**SCIENTIFIC NAME:** Amphibious reporticus
**QUOTE:** "Hi-ho, Kermit the Frog here."
**PHILOSOPHY:** It's not that easy bein' green—but it's all I ever really want to be.
**FAVORITE SONGS:** "Bein' Green"; "A Froggy Day"
**BEST FRIEND:** Grover
**LIKES:** Being the official Frog on the Street interviewer; fresh flies (when in season)
**DISLIKES:** Being eaten by interviewees; French chefs who stare at his long extremeties
**HOBBIES:** Playing the banjo; playing leapfrog (on the pro-amphibian circuit)

# KERMIT:
## frog on the street

Kermit is perhaps the only normal person on *Sesame Street*—except for the fact that he's a frog. He's funny, ironic, and always the voice of reason amidst the insanity around him; the calm in the eye of the storm. Whether he's trying to get to the true story behind a fairy tale or nursery rhyme gone awry, teaching us about a concept, a number, or a letter, or simply helping out a fellow Muppet (usually Grover), Kermit does it with humor, wit, and flair.

What is it that everyone loves about this green amphibian? For starters, he's caring. He's calm and tolerant, to a point—but he'll always tell you how he really feels. Whenever his lesson or interview goes amok, he tries to go with the flow—until he just can't take it anymore. Then, like us all, he cracks. He yells, flails his arms, and ultimately leaves us laughing out loud. Kermit's also the great straight man—er, frog—of the show. A sly glance to the camera and a subtle wrinkle of his mouth lets us know that he's fully aware of the craziness around him.

More than anything, Kermit is just plain *nice*. He understands. He knows what life is about, what's *really* important. He's genuine. He never lies or patronizes. And he only criticizes when absolutely necessary.

### KERMIT'S FAIRY TALE NEWS

Kermit the Frog, every bit as tenacious as Woodward and Bernstein, Mike Wallace, or Sam Donaldson, is *Sesame Street*'s intrepid roving reporter, the frog on the street. He truly personifies the term "beat news reporter"—for Kermit gets beaten down in just about every story he reports. Kermit specializes in ferreting out the true story behind our most beloved fairy tales or nursery rhymes. And the truth is not always what he expects. In fact, it never is. Here's a look at the stories he's broken. Or that have broken him, as the case may be.

### PETER PIPER

Kermit visits Peter Piper's pepper patch to interview Peter Piper as he picks a peck of pickled peppers, but only encounters Peter's relatives: Porter, Pepper, Porker, Piper, and several others. He never does meet Peter, but Kermit does learn that, as Porter puts it, "All we Pipers pick pickled peppers. We're pepper pickers. But Pete gets all the publicity. 'Scuse me—I gotta go pick a peck."

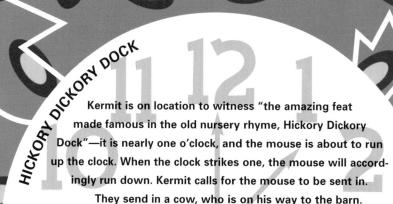

## HICKORY DICKORY DOCK

Kermit is on location to witness "the amazing feat made famous in the old nursery rhyme, Hickory Dickory Dock"—it is nearly one o'clock, and the mouse is about to run up the clock. When the clock strikes one, the mouse will accordingly run down. Kermit calls for the mouse to be sent in. They send in a cow, who is on his way to the barn. Next comes a duck. Kermit explains he's waiting for a mouse. The duck explains that he's looking for work, and asks, "Sure you wouldn't like a Hickory Dickory Duck?" Kermit tells the duck to beat it. Finally a horse arrives and explains that the mouse couldn't make it. He gallops toward the clock and crashes into it, forcing Kermit to say, "There you have it, folks. The horse ran up—uh, make that, through—the clock, the clock has just struck... seventeen, and what will happen next is... I'm getting outta here."

## THE OLD WOMAN WHO LIVES IN A SHOE

Kermit is looking for the famous old woman who lives in a shoe. He first stops at the house of the young man who lives in a glove—"If you knock on his door, he'd give you a shove. *(Shove)* Now get moving." Next Kermit finds the young woman who lived in a hat—"She could bark like a dog and meow like a cat!" At long last, he finds the old woman who lives in a shoe—and she ropes him into baby-sitting her many children while she goes out. It's bowling night!

## MARY HAD A LITTLE LAMB

Kermit interviews Mary at school about that nutty lamb that follows her around. The lamb doesn't have much to say, but does form a strong attachment to Kermit. In the end, the lamb follows Kermit home.

## HEY DIDDLE DIDDLE

Kermit's on the scene for the famous nursery rhyme "Hey Diddle Diddle," in which a cat is about to play the fiddle and a cow will make her famous jump over the moon. In the best sportscaster tradition, Kermit asks the cow why she wants to do it.

**Cow:** Because it's there. Because I want to prove that we cows can do anything we can set our minds to. People think we do nothin' but moo and give milk all day—but they're wrong.

The cow makes it, but crash-lands and destroys the grandstand, almost crushing Kermit. Nevertheless, as the cow puts it: "It's a small jump for cows, a giant leap for cowdom."

secret fact:

It's Not That Easy Bein' a Coat
Kermit's been around for much longer than many of us have been alive. He first appeared in Jim Henson's television show *Sam and Friends* back in 1955. Back then he was a lizard-looking fellow; he had no collar and no frog flippers (just regular Muppet feet). Believe it or not, he was originally constructed from Jim Henson's mother's spring coat, with two halves of a Ping-Pong ball for eyes.

Did You Know?
Kermit and Ernie are the only Muppets that are constructed with a built-in smile. All the other Muppets are built without expressions.

## PINOCCHIO

Observe the way in which our amiable amphibian teaches us that honesty really is the best policy after all in this classic sketch with everyone's favorite wooden boy, Pinocchio.

**Kermit:** Better stand back and get a wide picture because his nose grows and we don't want to blow it. The picture, that is, not the nose. Oh, are we on? Hi, ho, Kermit the Frog here in the shop of Gepetto the shoemaker with his famous little wooden boy, Pinocchio...It is said that when Pinocchio tells a lie, his nose gets longer. And when he tells the truth it gets shorter.

**Pinocchio:** Hey, Kermit, wanna see me lie and make my nose get longer?

**Kermit:** Would you?

**Pinocchio:** Sure. People come from all around to see this. *(Shouts out)* My name is Abraham Lincoln and I'm five hundred feet tall! *(Pinocchio's nose grows and catches Kermit's trenchcoat)*

**Kermit:** *(A little disturbed at being jostled by a nose)* Hey, it really did get longer. Talk about a nose for news, folks!

**Pinocchio:** You call that longer? I'll show you longer. This is longer. *(Shouts out)* I am a thousand million years old and I can lick superman! *(His nose grows pushing Kermit back again)*

**Kermit:** Uh, could you please tell the truth now and make it shorter, because I think your nose is caught in my coat....

**Pinocchio:** *(As Kermit protests while being pushed toward the wall, right)* And then I ate the whole world and then I sat on the moon and then I became President of the United States. *(Nose grows and Kermit is shoved against the wall)*

## SNOW WHITE

Kermit visits the castle of the Wicked Queen to interview

the magic mirror and to watch her ask her famous question, "Mirror Mirror, on the wall/ Who's the fairest one of all?"

You were expecting the Mirror to answer, "Snow White." Right? This time, the Wicked *(green)* Queen thinks she's got the Mirror beaten. With Kermit hiding in the wings, waiting to record the moment, the clever Queen points her mike at the mirror and asks:

"Mirror mirror, on the wall, who's the fairest of them all...who's the fairest of them all and is wearing a hat, has two beautiful eyes, is green, is in the same room with you right now, and is holding a

microphone.... Lay it on me!"

The Mirror answers, "Kermit the Frog."

Kermit is surprised, but flattered. "Me? Me? I'm the fairest? Oh really! Uh, well, thank you!" Disappointed, the Wicked Queen looks at Kermit, pauses, and then agrees with the Mirror that Kermit is pretty cute. She asks Kermit where he got his flippers. The tale ends with a lively discussion of Kermit's fetching attire.

## HUMPTY DUMPTY

**Kermit:** Hi-ho, this is Kermit the Frog speaking to you from the scene of the accident, where Mr. Humpty Dumpty has just fallen off his wall. And to recapitulate that story, you may remember that:

Humpty Dumpty sat on a wall
Humpty Dumpty had a great fall

And right now, some of the King's men, aided by a few of the King's horses, are attempting to put Humpty Dumpty together again. (A horse hurries by.) Excuse me, sir, I see you're one of the King's horses. Can you give our viewers a report on Humpty Dumpty's condition?

**Horse:** Well, uh, Dumpty's a tough egg. Not what you'd call hard-boiled, or anything, but he had a pretty bad fall. You can see part of him over there—and there's another part—and that's the rest of him there. (Horse hurries off to help others in background.)

**Kermit:** Yes, folks, it looks like a bad break for Mr. Dumpty, all right. But stay tuned, egg lovers, because the delicate job of putting Humpty Dumpty together again has started! Yes, I see that the bottom and the middle parts are already in place—and here comes the last part! They've done it! Humpty Dumpty has been put back together again. (Kermit goes over to interview him as the King's men and horses cheer and congratulate each other.) Tell me, Mr. Dumpty, how do you feel now that you've, uh, got it together again?

**Humpty:** I feel like a brand-new person.

**Kermit:** You heard it, folks. Although Mr. Dumpty went to pieces after falling off that wall, he's back to his old self again. (Turning to Humpty) It's nice to have you back. (Kermit slaps him on the back, and he falls of the wall again and breaks. Kermit looks around, calls for the King's horses and the King's men again, and sidles off-screen.)

# These fairy tales are beginning to get me down.
—Kermit the Frog

# RAPUNZEL, RAPUNZEL, LET DOWN YOUR HAIR MY HEAH?

### RAPUNZEL, *SESAME* STYLE

Kermit is at the witch's tower, where Rapunzel is held captive. Prince Charming is ready to make the big rescue.

**Rapunzel:** *(With a New York accent)* Get me outta heah!

**Prince Charming:** My love!

**Kermit:** *(To camera)* Isn't that beautiful? *(To Prince)* Pardon me, Prince, can you tell me—do you have a plan to rescue Princess Rapunzel?

**Prince Charming:** Yes.

**Kermit:** Would you mind telling us what your plan is? *(Nods enthusiastically at camera)*

**Prince Charming:** Yes.

**Kermit:** You do mind? You won't tell us?

**Prince Charming:** No way. Please! *(Pushes Kermit out of the way)* Rapunzel! Rapunzel! Let down your hair!

**Rapunzel:** What? Whaddya say? I can't hear yah! Can yah tawk loudah?

**Prince Charming:** *(Louder)* Rapunzel! Rapunzel! Let down your hair!

**Rapunzel:** *(Snatches off her long wig, revealing that she's bald. She tosses her hair down to the Prince.)* Now what?

*(Disgusted, the Prince leaves, and the fairy tale deteriorates from there.)*

## KERMIT ON FROGS

**Kermit:** Hi-ho, Kermit the Frog here. Today, we are going to talk about frogs. *(Bob enters with something cupped in his hands. Something large and green and slimy.)* Good heavens! What is that?

**Bob:** It's an American bullfrog, Kermit.

**Kermit:** *(To camera)* I'm more handsome than I realized.

*(Bob goes on to describe the frog to Kermit—he's green, he has strong legs.)*

**Kermit:** He's got a face that would stop a clock.

**Bob:** Why don't you tell everyone where frogs live, Kermit?

**Kermit:** *(With authority)* Frogs live in apartment houses with furniture and television sets and we sometimes have—

**Bob:** Uh, Kermit, most frogs don't live in apartments in the city. They live in riverbanks, ponds, even in swamps and mud holes.

**Kermit:** Mud holes! Why, that's terrible! If you lived in a mud hole, your floor would get dirty!

**Bob:** Kermit, what do frogs like to eat?

**Kermit:** Oh, that's easy. Fried chicken and pizza and pancakes and French fries.

*(Bob explains that most other frogs eat different things, like flies, worms, and spiders.)*

**Kermit:** *(Sickened)* If you excuse me, Bob, I think I have to lie down. I'm feeling a little nauseous. *(The bullfrog starts to croak.)* Wait a second, what's that? *(Kermit*

*starts listening to the frog.)* What's that? Oh, that's funny. *(Laughs)*

**Bob:** Wait—you mean to tell me, Kermit, that you understand what he's saying?

**Kermit:** Of course I do. I'm a frog.

**Pssst!!**

## secret fact:

### This Skit Has Been Brought to You by the Letter P

During the taping of this "Kermit and the bull-frog" bit, something happened that almost caused Jim Henson and Bob to blow it. According to Bob, he was holding the bullfrog over Jim Henson's head as Jim was manipulating Kermit. "I guess it was the first time for this frog on network television," Bob remembers. "He got nervous and did—what nervous frogs do. Right on Jim."

Bob didn't think that Jim would be able to keep his composure, but he did. They continued as if nothing had ever happened, and finished the bit. "It's just a horrible injustice that this giant American bullfrog would take that sort of an attitude with Kermit's best friend," Bob adds.

**P** Has sponsored show more than: 120 times

Has stood for:

Painting, Pillow, Ping-Pong, Pirate, Puppy, Pyramid

# THE FABULOUS FLEA CIRCUS (LETTER F)

*A fantastic way to learn about the function of that fun letter, F.*

**Announcer:** This is my fantastic flea circus, featuring the fabulous flea family, Freddie, Fats, Fannie, Filbert, and Floyd Flea.

**Filbert:** Floyd has the flu.

**Announcer:** Flu?

**Filbert:** So Fats will fill in for Floyd.

**Announcer:** Fine.

**Filbert:** Better make it fast, 'cause Fats has a five o'clock flight to Finland.

**Announcer:** Let's feature Fats first on the format, then.

**Filbert:** Fire away, Fats!

**Fats:** First, I fly the flag. Then, a flute fanfare, then I do a flying flip! Oh! Oh! I fractured my foot.

**Announcer:** Now featuring Freddie and Fannie Flea firing the field cannon on Fort Founter.

**Filbert:** Freddie and Fannie are feuding and refuse to perform.

**Announcer:** Ask Filbert to fill in!

**Filbert:** *I'm* Filbert!

**Announcer:** Listen, Filbert, you follow Fats and fire on the fort.

**Filbert:** Fine, fine. First I put the flame to the fuse and KABOOM!

**Announcer:** Filbert, you fool!

**Filbert:** Oh, phooey!

**Announcer:** Anybody wanna buy a used F?

**F** Has sponsored show more than: 150 times

Has stood for:

Face, Factory, Fairy, Fire, Flea, Frog

# Guy $miley

## I'll Take *Sesame Street's* Game Shows for $500, Guy

What could be more thrilling than winning a huge pot of money on *Jeopardy!* or *The Price Is Right*, hanging out with Alex Trebek and Bob Barker, meeting lovely spokesmodels—sounds like the most fun you could ever have, right?

*Wrong*! Those regular game shows are as dull as their home board-game versions if you compare them to the excitement of a Guy Smiley/Sonny Friendly/Pat Playjacks production. The guests on a *Sesame Street* game show get an experience they'd never trade for all the wheel-spinning and ceramic dalmatians in the world. "It ain't a party 'til something gets broke" was written for *Sesame Street* game shows. Practically every game show ends with the studio getting trashed.

Remember when Cookie Monster won on one of Guy Smiley's first shows—and chose a cookie instead of an all-expenses paid trip to Hawaii? Remember when Herry drove a bevy of cars into Guy's studio? Remember "Here is your life—Oak Tree" with Granny Fanny Nesslerode who raised the tree from a small acorn?

This is Guy Smiley, America's favorite game-show host of stupid game shows!
—Guy Smiley

We watched in amusement as the *Sesame Street* game-show host cried, hopped up and down in a rage, stood by nonplussed as his studio was demolished, and ultimately screamed for his limo to take him away. The game shows also gave us the opportunity to learn about everything from addition to rhyming, from the parts of the body to the life cycle of a tree.

Now for your reading, viewing, and remembering pleasure, here are some of *Sesame Street*'s best game-show moments. Ready? Hands on buzzers, please. Get ready to play along, and please don't forget to answer in the form of a question.

## THE ANYTHING-IN-THE-WORLD-PRIZE GAME

**Host:** Guy Smiley

**Contestant:** Oscar the Grouch

**Guy Smiley:** Hello, hello, hello, ladies and gentlemen. It's me, your favorite star of daytime television, Guy Smiley! We've taken our cameras out of the studios and out here to *Sesame Street* to play your favorite television quiz game, *The Anything-in-the-World-Prize Game*. Isn't that wonderful? All our contestant has to do is answer all three of our questions, and that contestant can have *anything in the world*—how about that? So now, let's welcome our first contestant, Mr. Oscar the Grouch! *(Knocks on Oscar's can. Oscar pops up.)*

**Oscar:** Look, I was just in the middle of a manicure, so if you— *(notices cameras)* Hey, what's all this?

**Guy:** These are cameras, Mr. Grouch. And as you well know, I'm Guy Smiley, star of daytime television, and this is *The Anything-in-the-World-Prize Game*.

**Oscar:** Peddle it somewhere else. I never watch TV.

**Guy:** All you have to do to win *anything in the world* that you want is to answer our three questions!

**Oscar:** Maybe you didn't understand—you can take your questions and—

**Guy:** *(Ignoring him)* Here's the first question, Mr. Grouch. And lucky you, it's an easy one. Are you ready? What is my name?

**Oscar:** *(To camera)* Who *is* this guy?

**Guy:** Who is this—*Guy*!!! Right! Guy Smiley is my *name*! One question right and two to go. Here is your next question. Can you give me a two-letter word, beginning with the letter N, that means...

**Oscar:** No!

**Guy:** Riiiiight! And I didn't even finish the question. That's two correct answers, and one more will make three. And we all know what *that* means, don't we, folks. Riiiiight! Anything in the world! So no help from the audience, please. Here is the third and last question: What happened to the man who went into the woods without a map!

**Oscar:** Get lost!

**Guy:** Get lost—what happened to the man who went into the woods without a map. And the correct answer is: Get lost! You have won *anything in the world*!!! The next words you speak can affect the rest of your life! Now that you can choose *anything in the world* that you want, what will it be?

**Oscar:** Get outta here!

**Guy:** Get outta here. You hear that, folks? An unusual but interesting request. This is Guy Smiley, star of daytime television, wrapping it up for today and saying so long for *The Anything-in-the-World-Prize Game*. *(Aside to the cameraman)* Come on, Arnie. I think we got off easy on that one.

**Oscar:** I have a feeling I blew an opportunity there.

# THE GAME-SHOW GALLERY

## BEAT THE TIME

**Host:** Guy Smiley

**Object:** To return with things that rhyme with "rain" before the clock runs out

**Contestant:** Cookie Monster

**How it went:** Cookie returned with a "cane" *(and an old man complaining about it)*; a "chain" *(to which a rabid monster was attached)*; a "train" *(with which he wrecked the studio)*.

**The Prize:** A cookie.

**The Inevitable Outcome:** Cookie trashes the studio, but "Beats the Time" and wins the cookie.

**Quote of the show:** "Hi, Guy."
—Cookie Monster

## THE CRYING GAME

**Host:** Sonny Friendly

**Object:** Sonny tells sad stories and the person who cries the most wins.

**Contestants:** Luke Warm, Ida Nomer *("Just call me Miss Nomer")*, Gordon Bleu.

**How it went:** Gordon Bleu looked as if he was going to win *(he lost it over a story about a restaurant that didn't serve croissants).*

**The Prize:** Sonny Friendly's teddy bear.

**The Inevitable Outcome:** Sonny is so sad about his teddy bear being the prize that he cries harder than anyone else, and wins.

**Quote of the show:** "No croissant? How can that be? Are we not civilized?" —Gordon Bleu

**Host:** Guy Smiley

**Object:** To answer every question asked with the response, "a triangle."

**Contestants:** Carl Mericana from Savana Montana, Prairie Dawn

**How it went:** Carl can't pull it together, so Prairie Dawn answers all of the questions "a triangle," despite her continued complaints about how stupid the game is.

**The Prize:** An all-expenses-paid trip to the Bermuda Triangle.

**The Inevitable Outcome:** Prairie wins, but thinks it's the stupidest game she's ever played.

**Quote of the show:**
"You just answer 'a triangle' to every question? That is a game? Not much of a game."
—Prairie Dawn

## SQUEAL OF FORTUNE

**Host:** Pat Playjacks

**Hostess:** Velma Blank

**Object:** To guess how many happy squeals the pig will make when you spin him around.

**Contestants:** Count von Count, Prairie Dawn

**How it went:** Prairie guesses ten squeals, The Count guesses five—the pig squeals five times.

**The Prizes:** A fifty-gallon barrel of gray-green industrial-strength fingerpaint, grapefruit goggles, and a larger-than-life portrait of Pat Playjacks.

**The Inevitable Outcome:** The Count wins, but doesn't want the prizes offered; he picks the pig instead.

**Quote of the show:** "It is so nice to be on a normal, sensible show like this." —Prairie Dawn

## HERE IS YOUR LIFE: SNEAKER!

**Host:** Guy Smiley

**Object:** To re-live the life of the honored guest, a used sneaker (right foot).

**Participants:** Rita Rucci (designer), Gyros Spiniapolis (shoemaker), Little Lizzy Hammertoe (wearer), Left (Right's former mate).

**How it went:** Sneaker is visited *(in moving detail)* by his designer, maker, the little girl who wore him, and his former mate, Lefty.

**The Prizes:** A memory book and an ankle bracelet.

**The Inevitable Outcome:** Oscar comes in and steals the sneaker to add to his rotten sneaker collection.

**Quote of the show:** "We used to walk to school together." —Sneaker

## THE ADDITION GAME

**Host:** Guy Smiley

**Object:** Solve the addition problems on the wall.

**Contestant:** Herry Monster

**How it went:** Herry solved all the problems except for the last one (3 + _ = 4) which he wanted to check out more closely—so he drove four cars into the studio, one at a time.

**The Prize:** An all-expenses-paid vacation to Malpitas, CA.

**The Inevitable Outcome:** The studio is a shambles.

**Quote of the show:** "Where did I lose control?" —Guy Smiley

## TO TELL A FACE

**Host:** Guy Smiley

**Object:** To recognize which person is a member of your family.

**Contestant:** Baby Bobby from Binghamton.

**How it went:** Guy introduces three choices for the baby's grandmother—a middle-aged man with a mustache and a gray wig, an old woman with gray hair, and a dog with a gray wig. The baby doesn't speak—he goos and gaas until he finally picks his grandmother.

**The Prize:** None—apparently Guy thinks recognition of a loved one is prize enough.

**The Inevitable Outcome:** The baby and grandmother are reunited and Guy Smiley leaves, looking for his limo.

**Quotes of the show:** "Gaa gaa goo!" —Baby Bobby; "You're absolutely riiiiiight!" —Guy Smiley

### OTHER PRIZES YOU CAN WIN ON A GUY SMILEY/SONNY FRIENDLY PRODUCTION

- A Guy Smiley Lunchbox
- A Guy Smiley Bookbag
- A Guy Smiley Thermos
- A Guy Smiley Pencil Set
- A Guy Smiley Coloring Book
- *The World According to Guy* (Guy's autobiography)

**BORN:** August 31 (Virgo)
Herry, like most Virgos, is a loner who likes to figure things out on his own, to feel useful, and to stay fit and healthy. But he often doesn't know his own strength, and usually ends up doing more damage than good. He shares his sign with Mother Teresa (who always did good), Lauren Bacall ("If you need me, just whistle. You know how to whistle, don't you Herry?"), and David Copperfield (who, like Herry, always has a few tricks up his sleeve).

**VOICE AND PUPPETRY:** Jerry Nelson
**SCIENTIFIC NAME:** Bigus softius
**QUOTE:** "Ooops."
**PHILOSOPHY:** The bigger they are, the softer they are.
**FAVORITE SONGS:** "Fuzzy and Blue"; "Big Time"; "Let's Get Physical"
**BEST FRIEND:** Grover
**LIKES:** Barbells; using his strength to be helpful; cute little baby animals
**DISLIKES:** When he scares people away
**HOBBIES:** Weight-lifting and doing needlepoint

*I don't like to brag, Gordon, but I was the cutest monster in my family.* —Herry

# A VERY
# HERRY
# MONSTER

Herry can always be counted on to help—although his brawny brand of assistance usually causes more problems than it solves. He's fuzzy and blue, big and burly, but he also has a gentle side. He's John Goodman on *Roseanne* and Lurch on *The Addams Family*—a bull in a china shop, a big softie at heart.

Herry doesn't know his own strength, but he nevertheless teaches that sometimes you can accomplish more if you just slow down, listen, and cooperate with others. He's also especially wonderful with children, and many of his classic bits on the show have involved John-John, Michael, and other young visitors. Here are a few of his memorable moments.

## CAN YOU KEEP A SECRET?

Herry and Grover taught us about secrets and the alphabet in this early skit.

**Herry:** *(To Grover)* Come here...

**Grover:** Did you call me?

**Herry:** Yeah. You wanna hear a secret?

**Grover:** A *secret*!

**Herry:** Shhhh!

**Grover:** *(Whispering)* Oh, yes! Yes, I would like to hear a secret.

**Herry:** Okay! Here it is—ABCDEFGHIJKLMNOPQRSTUVWXYZ! Shhhh! Don't spread it around! *(Leaves)*

**Grover:** Wow. Hey—Fenwick! Come here!

**Fenwick:** Yeah?

**Grover:** You'll never believe what Herry told me.

**Fenwick:** What?

**Grover:** He said ABCDEFGHIJKLMNOPQRSTUVWXYZ!

**Fenwick:** No kidding! Hey, Rosemary!

**Rosemary:** Did you call?

**Fenwick:** Grover says that Herry said, ABCDEFGHIJKLMNOPQRSTUVWXYZ!

**Rosemary:** Pamela! You've gotta hear this!

**Pamela:** What is it, dearie?

**Rosemary:** Fenwick says that Grover says that Herry says, ABCDEFGHIJKLMNOPQRSTUVWXYZ!

**Pamela:** Mercy!

**Rose:** Isn't it amazing?

**Grover:** But it's true! Herry said it! He said—

**All:** ABCDEFGHIJKLMNOPQRSTUVWXYZ! *(Herry returns as everyone is finishing the alphabet together)*

**Herry:** You're very good at reciting the alphabet, Grover—

**Grover:** Why, thank you!

**Herry:** —but you're lousy at keeping a secret.

## HERRY AND MICHAEL TALK ABOUT LOVE

Herry and Michael, one of *Sesame*'s young visitors, discuss the age-old subject of love in this sweet exchange.

**Herry:** Michael? I'm confused. Can you tell me what love means to you?

**Michael:** It means that a person likes somebody, and they hug and even kiss that person. And that's all love means.

**Herry:** Who are some people you love?

**Michael:** My mother, my father, my brother, and my sister.

**Herry:** Yeah. I love my mother and father and my sister and my brother, too. But there's somebody else I love. You! *(They hug)* 'Cause you're my good friend.

## HERRY AND JOHN-JOHN TALK ABOUT UP AND DOWN

**Herry:** Hey, John-John, do you know the difference between up and down?

**John-John:** I know it! Up is *(points up)* and down is *(points down)*!

**Herry:** Thank you, John-John. Gimme five! (*John-John slaps Herry five)* Save it for later!

**John-John:** Outta sight!

**Did You Know?**
Herry Monster is written to represent a monster with the psychological age of a six-year-old.

OSCAR
THE
GROUCH.

2. Beat it.

hike!

Shoo!

LEAVE ME ALONE
and leave!

Y rotten

# UNCANNED

**BORN:** June 1 (Gemini)
Oscar's dual Gemini personality keeps
him on his toes—he is either happy that he's
miserable or miserable that he's happy. He shares his
sign with Alanis Morissette (who has a similar problem),
Bob Dylan (who looks a little like Oscar, if you squint), and John
Kennedy ("Ask not what Oscar can do for you, but what you can
do for Oscar.")
**VOICE AND PUPPETRY:** Caroll Spinney
**SCIENTIFIC NAME:** Trashius mouthicus
**QUOTE:** "Scram!"
**PHILOSOPHY:** Leave me alone and I'll leave you alone.
**FAVORITE SONGS:** "I Love Trash"; "All You Need is Trash";
"I Wanna Hold Your Trash"
**FAVORITE MOVIES:** "The Dirty Dozen"; "Angels with Dirty Faces";
"Dirty Rotten Scoundrels"
**BEST FRIEND:** Slimey the Worm and Maria (though he wouldn't
admit it to her)
**LIKES:** Rainy days, arguing, standing in line at the
movies (not seeing movies, just standing in line);
anchovy milkshakes
**DISLIKES:** "You name it, I hate it.
Now go away."

Oscar is not a monster. Oscar is a grouch. What's more, he's the consummate pessimist. He's only happy if he's miserable. He loves to yell at people and tell them to leave him alone. But this often causes a dilemma. Because if people leave him alone, he has nobody to yell at. He also hates it when people are nice to him. But if people are truly nasty, Oscar has nothing to react against. He's stuck being—you guessed it—nice.

And there's the rub. Oscar is never satisfied. He sums it up best for himself: "Grouches don't like to be happy. If I'm happy I'm miserable—but I love to be miserable. So that makes me happy. But I don't like being happy. So that makes me miserable. But I love being miserable, so that makes me happy, but I don't like to be happy, so I get—you know, I'm a mess." Who says Prozac's just for humans?

Here are some of Oscar's trashier moments.

## WHAT'S IN OSCAR'S CAN:

A bowling alley

A goat

A piano

A pool with a dolphin named Ripper

A train set—"Grouch Central Station"

Chickens

Fluffy, the elephant, and her friends

## ROBERT MACNEIL INTERVIEWS OSCAR

Robert MacNeil has interviewed several *Sesame Street* characters over the years. In particular, he talked with Oscar about Oscar's "small business"—an ice-cream stand.

**MacNeil:** I see that you're in the ice-cream business.

**Oscar:** Oh, d'you figure that out all by yourself or did Lehrer help you? *(MacNeil asks Oscar what his "9 Delicious Flavors" are.)*

**Oscar:** Salami, Salmon Salad, Sardine, Sauerkraut, Sausage, Scallion, Sour Cream, Spaghetti, and Spare Rib.

**MacNeil:** You may have nine flavors, Oscar. But they don't sound delicious. In fact, if I may editorialize a little, and express my own opinion, they sound terrible, abysmal, and yucchy.

**Oscar:** Oh, yeah? Well, I don't like your tie.

> ### A lot of grouchy people really are not evil or bad in their heart. Oscar has a heart of gold.
> —Caroll Spinney

pssst!!

### secret fact:

How the Street Got its Grouch

The character of Oscar was inspired by a nasty waiter from a restaurant called Oscar's Tavern in Manhattan. Jim Henson and former *Sesame Street* director Jon Stone were waited on by a man who was so rude and grouchy that he surpassed annoying and started to actually amuse both Jim and Jon. They were so entertained that going to Oscar's Tavern became a sort of masochistic form of luncheon entertainment for them, and their waiter forever became immortalized as the world's most famous grouch.

> ### I always wanted Oscar to move into a nice, one-bedroom apartment.
> —Phil Donahue

## Oscar's Anthem

### I LOVE TRASH

Words and music by Jeff Moss
Copyright © 1970 Festival Attractions, Inc. (ASCAP)

Oh, I love trash
Anything dirty or dingy or dusty
Anything ragged or rotten or rusty
Oh, I love trash.
I have here a sneaker that's tattered and worn
It's all full of holes and the laces are torn,
A gift from my mother the day I was born
I love it because it's trash.
I have here some newspaper thirteen months old
I've wrapped fish inside it, it's smelly and cold
But I wouldn't trade it for a big pot of gold
I love it because it's trash.
I've a clock that won't work
and an old telephone,
A broken umbrella, a rusty trombone
And I am delighted
to call them my own
I love them because they're trash.

Oh, I love, I love, trash.

**pssst!!**

**secret fact:**
A Grouch is Born!
The voice of Oscar the Grouch was actually inspired by a cabdriver who drove Caroll Spinney to the studio during the first *Sesame Street* season. "Where to, mac?" the driver growled. Caroll thought the gruff voice was great, and tried it himself. He's been using it for Oscar ever since.

## OSCAR'S ROTTEN ABCS (WITH GROVER)

Only Oscar could turn the most innocent of alphabets into something truly rotten.

**Grover:** A is for Apple!

**Oscar:** B is for Blecchh!

**Grover:** C is for Cute!

**Oscar:** D is for Disgusting!

**Grover:** E is for Enjoy!

**Oscar:** F is for Frightful!

**Grover:** G is for Glad and also for Grover!

**Oscar:** H is for Horrible!

**Grover:** I is for Ice Cream!

**Oscar:** J is for Junk!

**Grover:** K is for Kiss!

**Oscar:** L is for Lousy!

**Grover:** M is for Marvelous and N is for Nice and I think everyone is marvelous and nice!

**Oscar:** O is for Oscar!

**Grover:** P is for Play!

**Oscar:** Q is for Quit it!

**Grover:** R is for Run!

**Oscar:** S is for Sickening!

**Grover:** T is for Terrific!

**Oscar:** U is for Ugly!

**Grover:** V is for Vanilla!

**Oscar:** W is for Worst!

**Grover:** X is for Xylophone!

**Oscar:** Y is for Yucchy and Z is for Zero, and that's what saying the alphabet with you is— yucchy and a great big zero!

**O** Has sponsored show more than: 210 times

Has stood for:
Oscar, Open, Opera, Orange, Orangutan, Over and Out

If there were another man in my life; it would be Oscar. Don't tell Luis.
—Sonia Manzano

## THE QUOTABLE GROUCH

**Oscar:** It's rotten to see you, Mom.

**Oscar's Mom:** That's nice of you, Oscar—is that any way to treat your Grouch mother? I knew *Sesame Street* would make you nice! How many times have I told you to argue with your mother!... I'm catching the next plane out of here.

**Oscar:** Rotten landings!

GROUCHES ARE BORN TO YELL.
—Oscar

## "MOM, CAN I SLEEP IN THE CAN TONIGHT?"

Caroll Spinney says that he's gotten several pictures from parents who've said, "This is a picture of my son. I had to buy him a trash can because he insists on being in the trash can while watching *Sesame Street*." And you thought *you* were a strange kid...

**SAT: SESAME ACHIEVEMENT TEST (GROUCH PORTION)**

**YOU CAN TELL A GROUCHKATEER BECAUSE _____.**

A ○ His thumb is always in his ear
B ○ He's always sure to compliment you on how bad you look
C ○ He's always willing to lend a helping foot
D ○ He looks like Bob.

*Answer: A. That way, no one can bother you!*

## TRASH CAN DRIVER: OSCAR MEETS JODIE FOSTER

**Jodie Foster:** Oscar, I have something important to tell you. I really like you a whole lot.

**Oscar:** You talkin' ta me?

**Jodie:** There's nobody else here.

**Oscar:** You call that important?

**Jodie:** Yes, I do—now, "important" is something that matters a whole lot to someone, and it's *important* for me to tell you that I like you.

**Oscar:** Well, it's not *important* to me!

**Jodie:** That's why I like you so much! I like you, Oscar, because you're a grouch, and

because you're not afraid to be different. Now, I think it's great that you don't think it's important to tell a friend that you like her.

**Oscar:** Not only do I think it's not important, I don't like it! I have something *important* to tell you—get lost!

*(Slams can shut)*

**Jodie:** I love it when he does that.

## STILL LIFE WITH TRASH CAN: THE ART OF OSCAR

There's an art to being a grouch. It has to do with the way you sneer, the way you insult your friends, the way nothing makes you happy. But mostly, it has to do with the art you create in your spare time. As the great art critic Vincent van Grouch said, his art isn't just bad— it's rotten.

*Still Life With Umbrella and Bananas* is one of Oscar's greatest works. But Oscar is uncharacteristically modest about his work. "You know I don't know art, but I know what I like—trash!"

*Fried Eggs on Toaster* is Oscar's obscure homage to the most important meal of the day.

*Whistler's Mud* is an eloquent statement about, well, mud. But as trash-art critic Vincent van Grouch once said, "This may be art, but it's not trash."

*Trash Can With Grouch* is without a doubt Oscar's masterpiece. After all, Oscar is an art form unto himself.

> ## Originally he was created as a character that would be a grouch and live in a trash can and come up and just go "Grrrrrrr!" again and again.
>
> —Jeff Moss, former *Sesame Street* head writer

---

**OSCAR'S ALWAYS HAD A WAY WITH WORDS, A PENCHANT FOR PET NAMES. SEE IF YOU CAN MATCH HIS NICKNAMES TO THE SESAME STREET PALS THEY REFER TO:**

1. Overgrown Bag of Giblets; aka Feather Face
2. Fur Face; aka Mount Rushmore
3. Mr. Badwrench
4. Music Puss, Tenor Face, and High Tonsils
5. Chrome Dome

A. Snuffy
B. Gordon
C. Bob
D. Luis
E. Big Bird

Answers: 1. E; 2. A; 3. D; 4. C; 5. B

## do you remember?

**Harvey Kneeslapper:** 'Scuze me—do you know where I wanna be?

**Anything Muppet:** I'm sorry?

**Harvey Kneeslapper:** I said, do you know where I wanna be?

**Anything Muppet:** No, I have no idea.

**Harvey Kneeslapper:** I wanna "B" right here! *(Slaps the letter B on the AM's sweater)* Heeheeheeheeeheee!

**B** Has sponsored show more than: 210 times

Has stood for:

Big Bird, Bubble gum, Banana, Ballerina, Broccoli, Bathtub

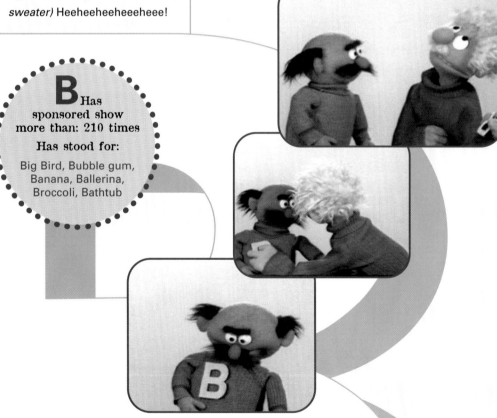

# MARVELOUS MARTHA

This is Martha.

Marvelous Martha, her mother calls her. Because Martha can print her own name.
Well, she knows the first letter.
Martha: "M."
Marvelous, Martha!

Martha: "M-M-M! M-M-M-M-M-M-M-M-M-Martha!"

## CECILLE THE BALL

She can bounce, she can roll
She can spin like a wheel

She's got a rubber soul
And her name is Cecille

Cecille, no one can match you
Cecille, you're off the wall
Cecille, I'm gonna catch you
And when I do I'm gonna have a ball!
Whoo!

chapter three

# Who Are the People in Your Neighborhood?
## The Cast

Oh, who are the people in
your neighborhood,
In your neighborhood,
In your neigh-bor-hood?
Oh, who are the people in
your neighborhood,
The people that you meet
each day?

"People in Your Neighborhood"
Words and music by Jeff Moss
Copyright © 1970 Festival Attractions,Inc.(ASCAP)

When you're three years old, the neighborhood where you live is more than a neighborhood—it's your world. And watching *Sesame Street*, children had the shared experience of growing up in a diverse, loving world full of people and creatures who cared about each other.

Let's admit it—when we were three, we all felt as if the people and creatures who lived on *Sesame Street* were our neighbors. We talked to the characters on the screen. We shouted out the answer when Susan or Bob sang "One of These Things. . ." We felt as if Mr. Hooper was our local proprietor, as if the Muppets were *our* best friends, too. In the *Sesame Street* neighborhood we had it all—our best friends, our first crush, our surrogate grandfathers and parents, our furry little companions—for at least an hour each day.

And they're still there, waiting to welcome you back. These are the people in our neighborhood, the people that we meet—and still love—each day.

Welcome back to the 'hood.

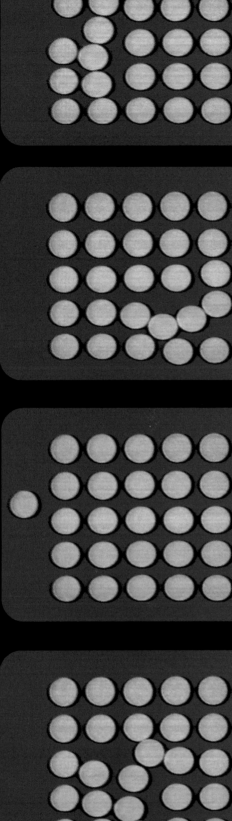

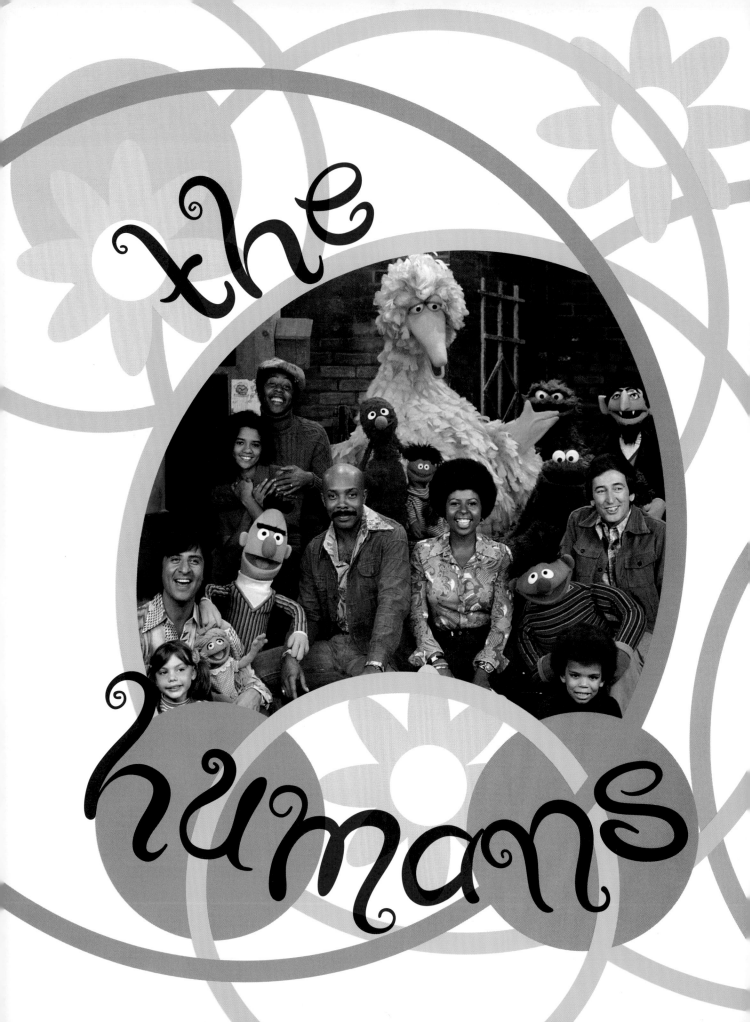

the

humans

Muppets, Muppets, Muppets! The Muppet characters seem to get all the glory, all the attention. Fans can quote Grover and Big Bird and Cookie Monster—they hear and imitate their voices—but how many of us can quote Bob, Mr. Hooper, Gordon, Susan, Maria, or Luis?

Everyone knows that *Sesame Street* wouldn't be the show it is today without the human characters. The humans are *essential* to the show—they're the ones who act as the fall guys, the guinea pigs for all the Muppets' shenanigans, the ones who take the pies in the face and get doused with water. The humans speak with the voices of reason—they explain things to Big Bird and Oscar, and thus, to us all.

So here's to the humans of *Sesame Street*, and to all the pies they took in the face, the silly costumes they wore, and the lives they live on the street.

> The grounding that this show has, one of the things that gives it some weight, are all the grown-up, adult human characters, and the simple reality the actors bring to their performances. But in comedy, the ones who play straight are rarely appreciated.
>
> —Norman Stiles, former *Sesame Street* head writer

# Maria

In 1974, a somewhat hippie-ish teen moved onto the Street, above Gordon and Susan's apartment. She flashed her infectious smile, got a job at the Lending Library (once housed where the Fix-It Shop is now, next to Hooper's), and immediately became a part of the family.

Sonia Manzano has played Maria ever since the character moved onto the Street. Many viewers watched her grow up. She was a first crush, a best friend, a baby-sitter. She told stories and made everyone laugh as Charlie Chaplin. She flirted (with David), was courted (by Luis), and then she married, had a baby, and raised her family.

## THE TRUTH REVEALED

Despite Internet rumors and what many fans believed to be true while they were growing up, Maria and Luis are *not* married in real life. According to Sonia Manzano, this is not an uncommon belief. One day, a woman recognized Sonia and Emilio Delgado, the actor who plays Luis, as they were walking down the street. She approached them and told them how great she thought it was that they fell in love *and* got married on television. "We're not really married," Sonia told her. They could see the disappointment in the woman's eyes, but the woman simply took a breath, paused, and said, "That's okay—as long as you really love each other."

**FULL NAME:** Maria Rodriguez (nee Figeuroa)
**PLAYED BY:** Sonia Manzano
**BORN IN:** Puerto Rico
**MARRIED TO:** Luis Rodriguez
**MOTHER OF:** Gabriela (played initially by Gabriela Reagan, Sonia's real-life daughter)
**VOCATION:** Co-owner/Manager of Fix-It Shop (specialty: toaster repair)
**BEST FRIEND (HUMAN):** Luis
**BEST FRIEND (MUPPET):** Oscar
**SUNNY PAST:** Starred in the original production of *Godspell*
**DEEP, DARK PAST:** Starred in Charles Bronson's *Deathwish*, and in the 1979 movie *Firepower*—died in both

## THE OTHER TRUTH REVEALED

Viewers can take solace in the fact that Maria's daughter on the show, Gabriela, *was* played by Sonia's real-life daughter, whose name just happens to be Gabriela, too. The real Gabriela left the show once she started kindergarten. "She didn't like to be the center of attention, which is what I thrive on," Sonia explains.

Sonia writes as well as acts for the show, and has earned seven Emmys for her writing. She was very involved in scripting Maria's marriage and pregnancy, and wrote the song "*Hola.*" Sonia says that she's always loved working on *Sesame Street*, and couldn't imagine ever having another job. "People would say, 'Don't you want to go on to other things?' Why? To do what? I can't think of doing anything more prestigious than *Sesame Street.*"

## CO-INCIDENCE, OR PSYCHIC FAME-NOMENON?

Sonia Manzano attended New York's famous High School of the Performing Arts—the high school where *Fame* took place. She attended the school with Northern Calloway, who played David on *Sesame Street*, and with Lou Berger, currently *Sesame Street*'s head writer.

At the beginning, the cast was really close. I mean we would party together, we would go out all the time. And I'm convinced that that makes great things happen.
—Sonia Manzano

Luis joined the street in 1971, and was the first human addition to the original cast. Bob was the storyteller and singer on the street, Gordon was the teacher, and Luis was the handyman, the Mr. Fix-It of the show. He's the one you'd probably most likely want to hang out with as an adult. He's also the dreamer on the show—a man who is ruled more by his heart than by practical considerations, an aspiring writer who is often in the middle of working on a children's book. He even sings and plays the guitar.

Luis, along with Maria, helps to teach viewers about Hispanic culture and language (remember when he couldn't find his way out of a brick room until he put the word *salida* up on the wall, and a door magically appeared?). With Maria, he also teaches viewers about love, courtship, and marriage. He made *agua* a household word. And whenever the toaster breaks, Luis is your man: "All we fix is toasters. That's what we do, man, we fix toasters. It's a joke, because nobody fixes a toaster, they just throw it away.... There's no money exchanged, but we're glad to fix your toasters.... "You break 'em, we take 'em,' that's our slogan."

To be sure, Luis and Maria must be known the world over as small appliance fixer-uppers. Robert Redford, Robert DeNiro, and Debra Winger have all dropped off toasters to be fixed on the show.

## DAVID WAS JILTED

What's the real story behind Maria and Luis getting married? Whatever happened to Maria and David?

Emilio doesn't know how to explain it. "A lot of people to this day ask me what happened, like Luis took Maria away from David. Before, there had been [a love] development between Maria and David—it wasn't overt, but they were like real close friends. Then all of a sudden, pop! There's Luis."

Emilio has been a professional actor for most of his life—he's also the only *Sesame Street* cast member from the West Coast. He's an actor first and foremost, and doesn't get too involved in story ideas or curriculum goals; however, he and Sonia Manzano are involved from time to time as consultants on the show's Latino curriculum.

### COMMERCIALS YOU CAN SEE EMILIO IN:

Nextel Cellular Phones, Denny's, Greyhound Bus

**FULL NAME:** Luis Rodriguez
**PLAYED BY:** Emilio Delgado
**BORN IN:** New Mexico
**MARRIED TO:** Maria Rodriguez
**FATHER OF:** Gabriela
**VOCATION:** Co-owner/Manager of Fix-It Shop (specialty—toaster repair; it runs in the family)
**BEST FRIEND (HUMAN):** Maria
**BEST FRIEND (MUPPET):** Big Bird
**SUNNY PAST:** Starred in the TV movie "I Will Fight No More Forever," the story of Chief Joseph; he played the Chief's brother, whose Indian name was "Frog." Also starred in *Cannon, Lou Grant,* and *Police Story.*
**DEEP, DARK PAST:** Starred in *Hawaii Five-0*

"We get paid to have fun. It's the best job in the world." —Emilio Delgado

# bob

*Sesame Street* just wouldn't be *Sesame Street* without Bob. Bob is always there, ready to sing, tell stories, explain something to Big Bird, and yes, to dress up like a bumble bee.

He's been there since the beginning, and his character hasn't changed much. When he first started the show, Bob asked the director who his character was supposed to act like. They told him to act like himself, and he's been acting like Bob ever since.

## "BOBU! BOBU!"

If things had been a little bit different, *Sesame Street* might not have had Bob for all these years. You see, Bob almost ended up a big star in Japan.

In the early 1960s, B.S. (Before *Sesame*) but after a stint with Leslie Uggams on the Mitch Miller show, Bob toured Japan, singing pop tunes (think Perry Como and Andy Williams) and discovered that he had quite a teenage following. Eventually, after more than eight hit albums and more than thirty hit singles, he toured to sellout crowds.

"In Japan, they'd scream 'Bobu! Bobu! Bobu Magulas!'" he says. "They claimed that if they shut their eyes they couldn't tell I wasn't Japanese." So Bob was offered the opportunity to move to Japan and pursue his career as a teen idol. But he passed up the chance because of his family.

## BOB, LIVE!

Bob still performs in many concerts and public appearances, particularly during the eight months when *Sesame Street* isn't taping. His stage show consists of a lot of *Sesame Street* music, as well as Broadway and movie theme songs that appeal to children. Look for him at a concert hall near you.

One day I was shopping in Sears and all of a sudden I felt this little hand holding onto my hand. I looked down and this teeny kid was holding on. I figured he'd probably grabbed the wrong hand thinking it was his father. So I looked down and said, "Hi." He said, "Hi," and kept holding right on. I said, "Do you know me?" He said, "Yep." I said, "What's my name?" He said "Bob." Like, idiot, don't you know your own name? And I said, "Oh. That's right. Do you know any of my other friends on *Sesame Street*?" He said, "Yep." And I said, "Who?" And he said, "Oh—number seven." Which really cracked me up, because I figured, hey, I'm right up there with the number seven.

—Bob McGrath

**FULL NAME:** Bob McGrath
**PLAYED BY:** Bob McGrath
**BORN IN:** Indiana
**VOCATION:** Private Music Teacher
**BEST FRIEND (HUMAN):** Linda
**BEST FRIENDS (MUPPET):** Big Bird and Oscar
**SUNNY PAST:** Was a featured "singalong guy" and tenor soloist on the Mitch Miller show
**DEEP, DARK PAST:** Author of *Uh Oh! Gotta Go!* and *Oops! Excuse Me Please!*
**ALBUMS:** "Sing Me a Story," "If You're Happy and You Know it—Sing Along with Bob," "The Baby Record," and many more

# David

David was the "cat in the hat" to viewers watching at home. He was that funny, upbeat, cool-looking guy. David gave advice, flirted with Maria, and taught everyone about the importance of good headgear. David was studying to be a lawyer, but when Mr. Hooper died, he took over Hooper's Store.

David was played by Northern Calloway, a talented stage actor who performed on and off Broadway for most of his life. He died in 1989.

**FULL NAME:** David
**PLAYED BY:** Northern Calloway
**BOYFRIEND OF:** Maria (until Luis made his guacamole for her)
**VOCATION:** Law student, then owner of Hooper's Store
**BEST FRIENDS (HUMAN):** Maria and Mr. Hooper
**BEST FRIEND (MUPPET):** Big Bird
**SUNNY PAST:** Starred in *Pippen*, replacing Ben Vereen on Broadway
**DEEP DARK PAST:** Had more hats than Queen Elizabeth

*Pssst!!*

secret fact:

The voice of Same-Sound Brown, a Muppet character who could rhyme absolutely anything, was also performed by Northern Calloway.

# Linda

**FULL NAME:** Linda Bove
**PLAYED BY:** Linda Bove
**VOCATION:** Librarian
**BEST FRIENDS (HUMAN):** Bob and Maria
**BEST FRIEND (MUPPET):** Barkley (he understands sign language, you know)
**SUNNY PAST:** Starred in *Children of a Lesser God*
**DEEP DARK PAST:** Played Fonzie's squeeze on *Happy Days*

Linda's role as *Sesame Street*'s deaf librarian is the longest-running role of any physically challenged person in a television series, and provides a positive role model for hearing and nonhearing children. She communicates with the other characters using sign language, but does also occasionally speak. Her pet dog, Barkley, understands certain sign language commands.

Linda has been played by Linda Bove since 1971 (she joined as a full-time Streeter in 1977). She has starred in *Children of a Lesser God* (in both a minor role in the film and as the lead in the national touring production) and *Search for Tomorrow*, and played one of Fonzie's "chicks" on *Happy Days*.

*Pssst!!*

secret fact:

*Sesame Street*'s writers once considered having Bob and Linda marry. Since Gordon and Susan, and Maria and Luis were already hitched, why not? Ultimately, however, Bob decided the married life wasn't for him—at least, not on television.

# GORDON

Matt Robinson

Hal Miller

**FULL NAME:** Gordon Robinson
**PLAYED BY:** Roscoe Orman
**BORN IN:** New York
**MARRIED TO:** Susan Robinson
**BROTHER TO:** Olivia
**VOCATION:** Originally an elementary school teacher, then became a high school teacher
**BEST FRIEND (HUMAN):** Bob (he taught Gordon to play the flute)
**BEST FRIEND (MUPPET):** Elmo (they exercise together)
**SUNNY PAST:** Roscoe has appeared in *All My Children, Kojak, Sanford and Son,* several films, and on Broadway in the award-winning *Fences*
**DEEP, DARK PAST:** In addition to playing "good guy" Gordon, Roscoe has also played many bad guys in films—including the title role in the 1974 film *Willie Dynamite*

## WILL THE REAL GORDON PLEASE STAND UP?

Gordon's a strong male role model, caring and competent—a man who loves sports and music, who can be firm but also soft and gentle. He's a teacher and an all-around good guy. Gordon's the one you'd go to for help if you were really in trouble.

In case you hadn't noticed, Gordon's changed a bit over the years—he's been played by three different actors. From 1969 to 1971, he was played by Matt Robinson, who looked a bit leaner than Gordon does today, had a bit more hair and walked and talked with a more streetwise flair. From 1971 to 1973, the role was played by Hal Miller; Gordon lost his trademark mustache, and seemed to gain a bit of weight. Then, in 1973, Gordon changed again. The mustache was back, he sported a more athletic build and he had less hair. This was the Gordon who was here to stay.

Actually, if things had gone differently, we might have ended up with a Gordon who looked an awful lot like Benson DuBois from *Benson.* Robert Guillaume, who went on to play Benson, was up against Roscoe Orman for the part of Gordon. Roscoe thinks that Guillaume is a great actor, but wasn't worried about losing the role to him: "He doesn't have that... *Gordon thing* that people like."

**Pssst!!**

secret fact:
Roscoe did the voice for Hardhead Henry Harris, one of the students in Roosevelt's class at Roosevelt Franklin Elementary School.

## LIKE FATHER, LIKE SON

In Season 17, Gordon and Susan adopted a son, Miles. This event came to be after Caroll Spinney (who plays Big Bird and Oscar), mentioned to his wife, Debra, that Roscoe Orman and his wife were having another child. Both Caroll and Debra then went to Dulcie Singer, the producer at the time, and suggested that Gordon and Susan have a child on the show, and that Roscoe's real son (Miles Orman) play the role. Miles Orman had the role of Miles Robinson until he was seven years old. Today, Miles Robinson is played by Imani Patterson.

*I had never worked with puppets before, so just the concept of talking to this green, grungy-lookin' rag comin' out of a trash can was totally alien to me.*
—Roscoe Orman

# Susan

On-screen, Susan is the mother of the show. She's the one who took care of Big Bird in the early days, the maternal figure who comforted and explained things to him and to all the viewers. She told Big Bird to go to bed and eat his birdseed and that everything was going to be all right. She also made the best milk and cookies. She was everyone's surrogate mother for an hour each day, and has been for more than thirty years.

## WHAT YOU DIDN'T KNOW ABOUT SUSAN

❁ She's played by Dr. Loretta Long, who received her Ph.D. in Urban Education in 1973 from the University of Massachusetts (she had already been on the show for four years).

❁ Susan, along with Bob and Big Bird, is one of only three cast members who were on the first show and have been played by the same actors since the show began.

❁ Susan grew up on a farm in Michigan, like Loretta.

*Pssst!!*

## secret fact:

Gordon and Susan never had last names until baby Miles came along. When they adopted Miles, they needed a last name for the adoption certificate. That's when they selected "Robinson," in honor of Matt Robinson, who played the first Gordon on the show.

## NOW WHAT?

Over the years, Susan's role has evolved from captain of the milk-and-cookie brigade into the broader role of nurse and homemaker. Loretta explains that the National Organization for Women played a big role in helping to make that career switch.

In the early days, NOW monitored the role of women on the show (at that time, just Susan). NOW carefully observed who initiated the action in various scenes (was it Bob, Gordon, Susan, or Mr. Hooper?) and who held the authority in the marriage (was it Gordon or Susan?). After the show had been on for several months, NOW presented its findings to the directors, producers, and writers of *Sesame Street*—and showed them how they had marginalized the character of Susan.

"After they presented their observations and concerns about our institutionalizing stereotypes," Loretta explains, "Jon Stone [the director] said, 'Well, let's give Susan a career.'" So she became a public health nurse and ran immunization clinics on the show with Maria's help.

During the early days, Loretta herself was also a substitute teacher in Bronx, New York. This was particularly confusing for the children she taught, who would often see her on television before school and in class later that day. Loretta still teaches at Roan University in New Jersey; and one of her classes is "The *Sesame Street* Approach to Elementary Education."

**"In 1969 we didn't even have words for what we're calling 'multicultural' now. We were doing it. It wasn't Dick and Jane's old neighborhood, with single-family houses and picket fences. It showed the inner city as being a place where people lived and loved each other and went to work. And in 1969 that was quite a concept."**
—Loretta Long

**FULL NAME:** Susan Robinson
**PLAYED BY:** Loretta Long
**BORN IN:** Michigan
**MARRIED TO:** Gordon Robinson
**MOTHER OF:** Miles
**VOCATION:** Public Health Nurse
**BEST FRIENDS (HUMAN):** Gordon and Maria
**BEST FRIEND (MUPPET):** Big Bird
**SUNNY PAST:** Before joining the cast she hosted *Soul*, a PBS variety show.
**DEEP, DARK PAST:** Taught as a substitute teacher during the first season of *Sesame Street*

Mr. Hooper was the grandfather of the Street. He was the wise old owl, the sweet but slightly crusty sage, the store-keeper you'd have gone to for advice—or for a good, stiff birdseed milkshake.

Hooper's Store is what all good communities and neighborhoods require—a gathering place. Hooper's Store is to *Sesame Street* what Cheers was to *Cheers*, what The Pirate's Cove was to *The Love Boat*, what Arnold's was to *Happy Days*: a place where Muppets and humans alike could go to get whatever they needed, whether that be a Figgy Fizz soda or a chocolate egg-cream (Hooper's specialty).

Will Lee, the actor who played Mr. Hooper, died in 1982. Will's passing compelled the writers to deal with the subject of death in an honest, moving way. "I'll miss you, Mr. Hooper," said Big Bird at the end of that segment. And millions still do.

# mr. hooper

### WHAT'S IN A NAME?

Big Bird never could get his old pal Mr. Hooper's name right. Here are some of the Bird's more memorable attempts:

Mr. Looper, Mr. Blooper, Mr. Duper, Mr. Snooper, Mr. Pooper, Mr. Scooper (but never "Pooper" and "Scooper" at the same time).

**One day I walked in and said, "Hullo Mr. Cunningham—oh gee, I wasn't even close."**
—Big Bird

**FULL NAME:** Harold Hooper
**PLAYED BY:** Will Lee
**BORN IN:** New York
**GRANDFATHER FIGURE TO:** Big Bird
**VOCATION:** Owner and proprietor of Hooper's Store
**BEST FRIEND (HUMAN):** Bob
**BEST FRIEND (MUPPET):** Big Bird
**SUNNY PAST:** Starred in Alfred Hitchcock's *Saboteur*
**DEEP, DARK PAST:** Once played a pinball maniac in a stage version of William Saroyan's *The Time of Your Life*

**psssst!!**
secret fact:
Mr. Hooper didn't have a first name until an episode in which he received his GED certificate for attending night school (he had never graduated from high school). On the diploma, he became "Harold Hooper."

## Olivia

Olivia was Gordon's sister on the show. She first appeared in 1976, and allowed the writers to show how family members relate to each other when they become adults (she and Gordon became good role models for younger brothers and sisters). Olivia was a photographer on *Sesame Street* but left the show in 1988.

Alaina Reed, who played the role of Olivia, is a stage actress and singer who has appeared in many on and off Broadway plays (including the national touring company of *Hair*). Reed also performs in nightclubs around the country.

## Buffy

Buffy was the only folk singer/songwriter to join the permanent cast of *Sesame Street*, even though several others (including Pete Seeger, Joan Baez, and James Taylor) have made special appearances. She joined the show in 1976 as the first Native American cast member, and taught us about the Native American culture and lifestyle.

Buffy was played by Buffy St. Marie Wolfchild, a native of Saskatchewan, Canada, whose songs have been recorded by Elvis Presley, Cher, Barbra Streisand, and Johnny Mathis. She wrote many of her own songs for the show, including "C is for Cody," "The Muskrat Song," and "I'm Gonna Be a Country Girl Again."

## Willy

Willy was the local hot-dog vendor played by Kermit Love, one of the original Muppet designers. Kermit is responsible for designing Big Bird's costume (although Jim Henson originally had the idea for the puppet) and for giving many of the Muppets the look we know and love. In case you're wondering, Kermit the Frog was *not* named after Kermit Love—it's just a coincidence.

## Mr. MacIntosh

Mr. MacIntosh was the local fruit and vegetable man and closet soft-shoe dancer (played by Chet O'Brien) who appeared intermittently from 1975 to 1992. An old-time vaudeville actor, Chet was also the *Sesame Street* floor manager. His twin brother, Snooks O'Brien, was the show's stage manager.

# mr. HandQorQ

Mr. Handford came to *Sesame Street* in 1989 to run Hooper's Store, a retired firefighter who bought Hooper's Store because he was "tired of being retired." Big Bird doesn't get *his* name wrong, but Snuffy and Alice do occasionally call him "Mr. Handfoot."

Mr. Handford is played by David Langston Smyrl, a character actor, comic, writer, and musician who was once crowned "Poet Laureate of Greenwich Village."

# Gina

Gina started on the show in 1987 as a teenager who worked in Hooper's Store. The young Gina enjoyed rock music (her musical idol is Little Jerry of Little Jerry and the Monotones) and acted as a big sister to many of the young Muppets. Recently, Gina ran a day-care center, where she cared for the Muppets.

Gina is played by Alison Bartlett, who joined the show in 1987. Bartlett has played on and off Broadway (she costarred with William Hurt and Candice Bergen in *Hurly-Burly*, directed by Mike Nichols), and also starred in the film *Right to Kill*.

# ruthie

Ruthie is the owner of Finder's Keepers, the thrift shop located around the corner from 123 Sesame Street. Her shop contains many magical things that help her to tell stories—including Old King Cole's crown and Little Jack Horner's horn.

She's played by Ruth Buzzi, star of *Laugh-In*, *That Girl*, and many other television shows. She's also starred in several films and on Broadway.

# uncle wally

Well, I'll be a musician's uncle! Uncle Wally visited the show as Bob's uncle from 1984 to 1992. The character was played by Bill McCutcheon, a Tony award-winning actor who has also been in several films, including *Steel Magnolias*.

# savion

Savion Glover, who played a street-savvy teenager on *Sesame Street*, made many guest appearances before becoming a cast member in 1990. Savion was a close friend of Gina's, as well as resident dancer-extraordinaire. In fact, he was such a spirited dancer that even between takes on the set, he just kept on tapping. Savion Glover is a veteran performer who made his Broadway debut at the age of twelve as the title character in *The Tap Dance Kid*. He was also nominated for his first Tony at the age of fourteen for his performance in *Black and Blue,* and later choreographed and danced in Broadway's *Bring in Da Noise, Bring in Da Funk*.

# lillian

Best known as the fun-loving woman who adores children, Mrs. Lillian Edwards ran the family day-care unit on the Street for three years.

Played by Lillias White, Lillian was a mature and positive role model for children. She is known now for her melodic voice as the lead muse in the *Hercules* movie.

# celina

A cast member for four years, Annette Calud as Celina owned and ran the dance studio located above the thrift shop, "Finders Keepers." Celina often held dance recitals to give her Muppet and human students a chance to perform. She herself once dressed as a broccoli and danced before an audience. Before *Sesame Street*, Annette starred on Broadway in the hit musical *Miss Saigon*.

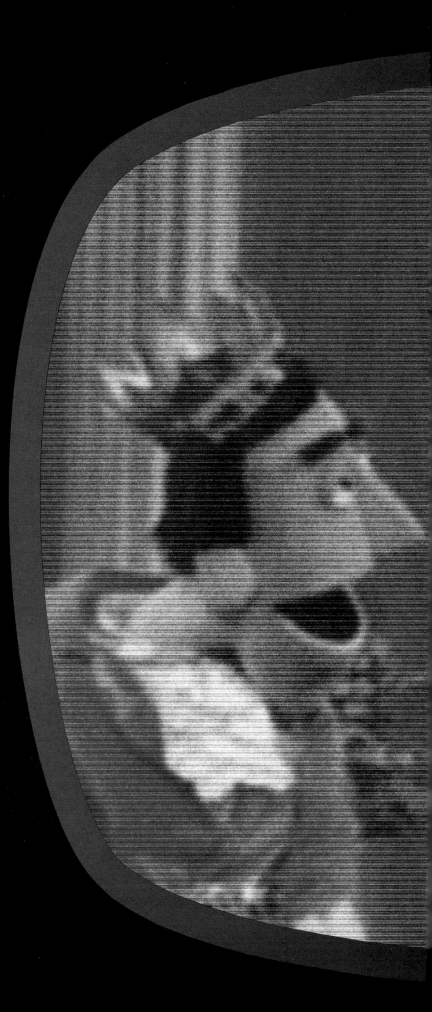

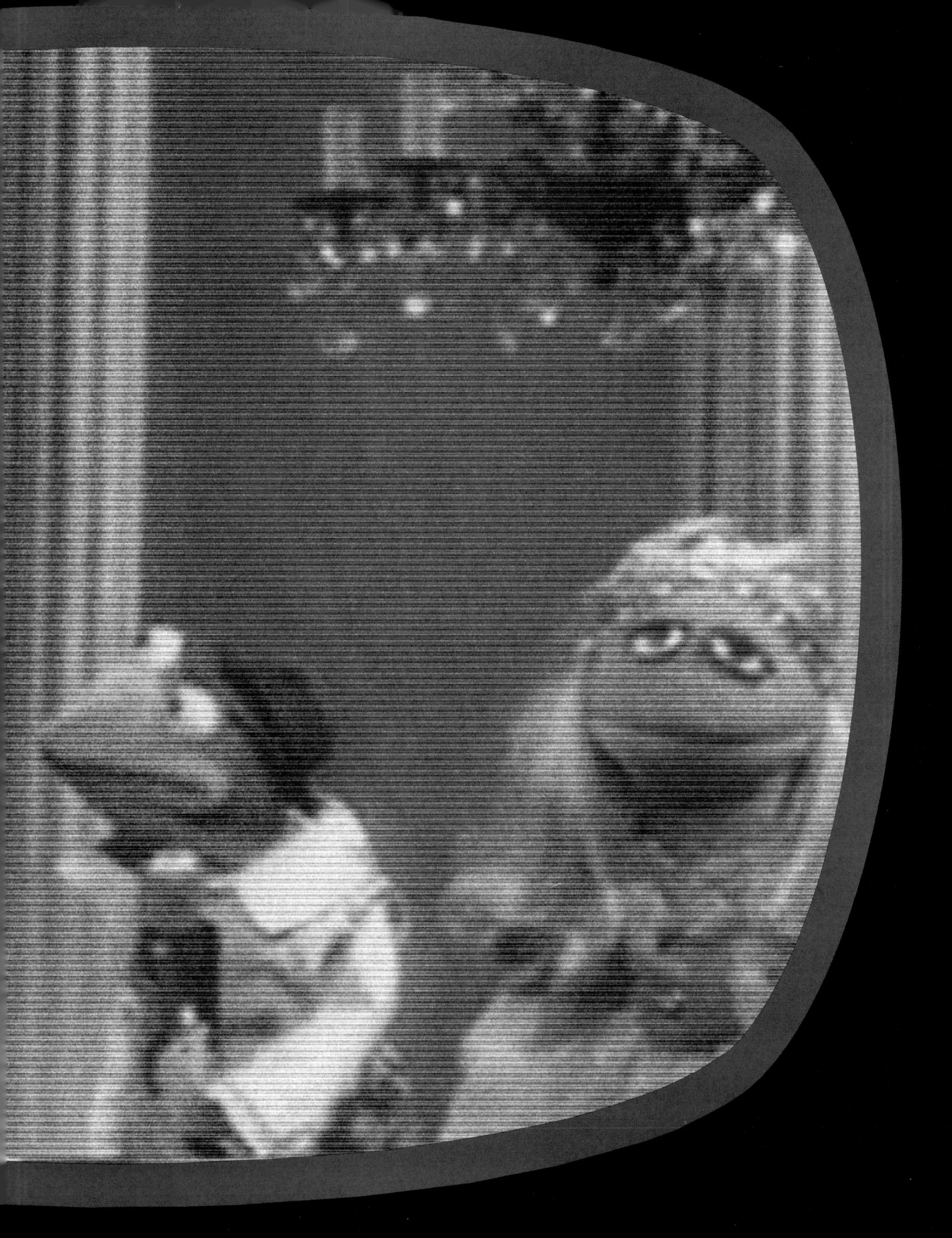

# THE ANYTHING MUPPETS

The group of nameless and faceless Muppets who can become anything, anywhere, at any time. They are the people in your neighborhood, the extras in the skits, the Muppet chorus line, or Greek chorus. Able to be used in an endless variety of combinations, the AMs (as they're called in the studio) have interchangeable features.

# MORE
## MUPPETS

### Alice Snuffleupagus

Snuffy's two-year-old sister, who is just learning about the world. She does whatever her brother does. She's half Snuffy's size and is worked by a single puppeteer—Judy Sladky. Her eyes and mouth are remote controlled, as Judy uses her arms and legs to work Alice's legs.

### Betty Lou

With her blonde braided hair, Betty Lou is friendly and unassuming. She likes to play and will always join her friends in a good game at the playground. She's happy to lend a helping hand. A doll aficionado, she has many dolls of various ethnicities and shapes, but she has one favorite that she carries with her everywhere. She is played by Lisa Buckley.

### Bruno

The silent Muppet trashman who carries Oscar around when Oscar needs to travel and talk at the same time. Caroll Spinney performs Bruno, and in fact invented the character as a way to "mobilize" Oscar.

### Buster the Horse

Forgetful Jones's intelligent horse and frequent savior. Also has a personality and life separate from Forgetful Jones—he often appears on the street to teach vocabulary, or to explain what foods keep him "healthy as a horse."

### Colambo

A black lamb detective who is reminiscent of TV's seemingly nonthreatening, trench coat-sportin' Lt. Columbo. Played by Joey Mazzarino, Colambo once helped Kevin Kline as Nick the Chicken solve the mystery of the missing chickens.

### The Countess von Backwards

The Count's girlfriend who shares his passion for numbers—except that she likes to count in reverse order. Her completed counting is always accompanied by a wolf's howl. Camille Bonora brings this cheerful vampire to life.

### The Countess (aka The Countess Dahling von Dahling)

The Count's other girlfriend (talk about a two-timer!) who worked with the famous German director Josef von Sternberg. Fran Brill, who plays her, says, "She is modeled after Marlene Dietrich and is in a committed relationship with The Count, but is still waiting for him to pop the question."

### Grungetta

Oscar's grouchy girlfriend, who shares "Oskie's" temperament for all things junky, rainy, and nasty—she's especially partial to tattered hats and veils. Grungetta is played by Pam Arciero.

### Sherlock Hemlock

The Muppet detective who solves mysteries by concentrating on the little clues and overlooking the big ones. He has worked to solve mysteries like "The Case of the Missing Half-a-Chicken Sandwich" and "The Case of the Missing Duckie." Muppeteer Jerry Nelson bases his performance as Sherlock on Basil Rathbone's movie portrayal of Sherlock Holmes.

## The Amazing Mumford

The W.C. Fields-esque magician who's great at magic—just not so great at predicting how his tricks will turn out. His trademark magic words, "A-là-peanut-butter-sandwiches," often produce more magic than he bargains for. Houdini unchained, he's played by Jerry Nelson.

## Forgetful Jones

The forgettin'est cowboy in the Wild Wild West. He helps us learn how to remember things we've, well, forgotten. But mostly he entertains us with his antics. Think Woody from *Cheers*, or Ted from *Mary Tyler Moore*. Forgetful was played by Richard Hunt, whose interpretation won't soon be forgotten.

## Barkley the Dog

Linda's pet—a large, friendly, shaggy dog who understands **the sign language commands for** "sit" and "stay." Barkley is performed by Bruce Connelly and does not speak, but is a darn good barker. He was originally named Woof-Woof and joined the cast full-time in 1978.

## Slimey the Worm

Oscar's mostly silent but always friendly pet worm. This worm-of-few-words received a lot of attention last year for his trip to the moon with WASA (the Worm Air and Space Administration). Slimey is also famous for his "worm tricks," such as diving from a trash can into a thimble of water. The worm is manipulated by Martin Robinson, who sums up Slimey best: "He speaks volumes in his eloquent silence."

## Little Bird

Big Bird's little friend, who is good at explaining concepts such as "Imagination" and "Next to." As played by Fran Brill, Little Bird is slightly wiser than Big Bird—sort of like Scrappy Doo to Big Bird's Scooby Doo.

## Rosita

A good-natured, intelli-**gent turquoise Muppet** who speaks in both English and Spanish, her native language. She's the first bilingual **Muppet ever to appear on the show.** She's played by Carmen Osbahr, who came from Mexico City where she worked on *Plaza Sesamo*.

**ssst!!**

### secret fact:

Rosita was originally conceived of as a fruit bat. Her full name is Rosita, La Monstrua de las Cuevas (The Monster of the Caves). Look closely—the girl's got wings!

## Baby Bear

**The character from that** Goldilocks story, in Muppet form. David Rudman plays Baby Bear with a babyish lisp. He's sometimes the too-cute little kid of the show—your Punky Brewster, your Emmanuel Lewis, your Olse

## Kingston Livingston III

A young African-American boy, he's friends with Roxy Marie. He's very smart and very cool and tends not to run with the pack, preferring his own unique style and point of view. He is performed by Kevin Clash.

## Natasha

The infant monster who speaks only in gurgles and is performed by Muppeteer Kevin Clash. She's also a fast crawler, making life difficult for her hapless baby-sitters. Mother Ingrid and father Humphrey are the proud parents of this fun-loving baby.

## Sherry Netherland

Sherry's the Leona Helmsley of the Furry Arms Hotel. She's a grande dame who wants her guests to be happy no matter what, and who can't say no to a guest's requests (even if they're ridiculous, which they usually are). She rules with an iron hand, a heart of gold, and a brain of oatmeal. She's played by Alice Dinnean.

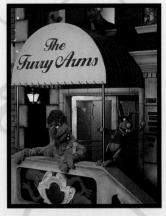

## Prince Charming

Guy Smiley in prince's clothing. He's so self-involved that he often abandons his role as the savior in Muppet fairy tales to satisfy his own needs. For example, he desperately wanted to find Cinderella, not because he loved her, but because he loved her glass slippers and wanted the other shoe. Look out, Imelda. Played by Frank Oz.

## Twiddlebugs

"Those are sweet little things, those Twiddlebugs are," says Ernie of the high-pitched family that lives in his flower box. Tina, Thomas, Teddy, and Tessie Twiddlebug are cute and innovative. They use tiny found objects for their furniture and toys. As played by Jerry Nelson, Frank Oz, Martin Robinson (and many others), they'll ensure that you never look at a stray button or thimble the same way again.

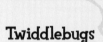

## The Honkers and the Dingers

A fun-loving team of nonverbal Muppets who honk (or ding, as the case may be) to communicate. Good to have around in a traffic jam, they're played by whichever Muppeteers happen to be on the set that day.

## Sonny Friendly,
### "America's Friendliest Game-show Host"

Host of such shows as "Squeal of Fortune," Sonny Friendly rivals Guy Smiley in obsequiousness. Richard Hunt made this Muppet the Pat Sajak of the show (whom he remarkably resembles). He's now played by David Rudman.

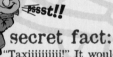

secret fact:
"Taxiiiiiiiiii!" It would take three days for a Twiddlebug to walk down *Sesame Street*.

## Two-Headed Monster

The twin monsters of *Sesame Street* who happen to share the same body. They speak to each other in a baby-like language that is mostly monster gibberish. They frequently need to cooperate, and can teach us how to do just that. Jerry Nelson and Richard Hunt originally played the creatures. David Rudman has since taken over Richard's role.

## Biff and Sully

Sully's the construction worker who works with Biff, the one who doesn't speak because Biff won't let him get a word in edgewise. Sully usually completes the projects before Biff can even fig-

ure out how to start them. Biff's a construction worker who acts like a know-it-all but is wrong most of the time. He's impatient with Sully and rarely notices that his partner's the one completing whatever task is at hand. Sully was played by Richard Hunt; Biff is performed by Jerry Nelson.

## The Martians

Interplanetary visitors who valiantly explore the world around them, despite the fact that they're constantly encountering things that terrify them—like telephones and clocks. "Yip-yipped" by Jim Henson, Jerry Nelson, and Martin Robinson.

## Fred the Wonder Horse

Marshal Grover's trusty companion, Fred's "horse sense" is always better than Marshal Grover's "Monster Sense." And Fred usually saves the day. Played by Jerry Nelson, Fred is Starsky to Grover's Hutch.

### VEGETABLES ARE MUPPETS, TOO!

We've met a lot of Muppets over the years—frogs, penguins, monsters, cows, letters, and numbers—but among the strangest Muppets of all are the talking foods that sometimes visit the street. It's enough to make you a carnivore.

## Gladys the Cow

A theatrical ham (even though she's a cow), she'll try out for any part in any theatrical production, whether or not she's right for the part. Richard Hunt was the Muppeteer who gave Gladys her piercing operatic voice.

## Fat Blue

The long-suffering Charlie's Restaurant customer who always has the misfortune of getting the eager-to-please Grover as his waiter. Played with tolerance by Jerry Nelson.

# WHAT-HAPPENED EVER TO...?

Whatever happened to those Muppet characters who once graced the small screen but have since gone on to join the cast of great has-beens, legendary Muppets like Roosevelt Franklin and Harvey Kneeslapper? Why were they eliminated? Did they offend the Bird? Were they once caught napping in Kermit's dressing room? Here are a few long-gone favorites, and why they're no longer around.

## Harvey Kneeslapper

The wild-eyed, laugh-happy blond Muppet who loved puns and played jokes on anyone he came across. Performed by Frank Oz, the character was chucked because he was a one-note joker, and because his constant laughing was too hard on Frank's voice.

An example of Harvey's antics:

**Harvey:** Do you want one? Hee hee hmmph! (Covers mouth in laughter)

**Ernie:** Sure!

**Harvey:** (Slaps the number one on Ernie's chest) There you go! (Laughs uncontrollably)

## Roosevelt Franklin

A little purple Anything Muppet who was originated and performed (voice only) by Matt Robinson. He attended Roosevelt Franklin Elementary School.

The precocious little purple Muppet was so popular that he even released his own album—*Roosevelt Franklin Sings*. Besides the basic curriculum concepts, Roosevelt taught us about family, about pride, and about respecting ourselves and others.

The character was abandoned because he was thought by some to be a negative cultural stereotype and because the schoolroom in which he spent most of his time was considered too rowdy and a bad example. The kids in the class (including Hard Head Henry, Smart Tina, and Baby Bree Boo Bop a Doo) were prone to smart-aleck remarks, throwing papers, and general disruptive class-room behavior. Nevertheless, Roosevelt remains an old *Sesame* favorite, and goes down in history as one of the coolest Muppet poets. (See page 162 for poems.)

**psst!!**

## secret fact:

The voice of Roosevelt Franklin's mother was performed by Loretta Long, who plays Susan on the show. Roosevelt Franklin was played by Matt Robinson, who played the first Gordon on the show.

## Simon Soundman

"I was wondering if I can use your *ring-ring*. You see, I was out riding in my *vvv-rooom, vvv-room* because I wanted to take my *waaaa! waaaa!* out to the country and show him a *cluck-cluck*, and a *mooo*, and a *neighhhh*, and an *oink-oink*. But I had to *screeeech* because a *choo-choo* was crossing the road. Then, when I went to go, I couldn't get *whir-whirr-whirrr*, so I *clomp-clomped* to your house, and now I would like to use your *ring-ring* to call the garage to fix my car."

## Professor Hastings

A professorial Muppet whose lectures were so dull that he put himself to sleep as he was giving them. While he was sleeping, whatever concept he was discussing would be demonstrated in the background (if he was talking about feelings, a group of "Happy" Muppets would walk through, for example). He was played by Frank Oz, but he didn't make the cut because he was, well, too dull.

## Sam the Super-Automated Robot

Played by Jerry Nelson who was boxed into a cumbersome suit, Sam was a robot who was supposed to answer and satisfy all our needs, but he always somehow got the answers wrong. If he was meant to make coffee he'd pour it with the cup upside down. If he was supposed to draw a circle he'd draw a square. And if he was supposed to be a hit, he wasn't.

## Don Music

The stressed-out songwriter with the mop top who always had trouble with the next line—"ABCDEF... EF... EF... Oh, I'll never get this song right, never, never, never!" Then he'd slam his head on the piano in utter frustration. The character, played by Richard Hunt, was abandoned because of complaints about his alarming tendencies toward self-inflicted punishment. Apparently, kids were imitating his head-banging at home.

# WANTED

# BAD BART

## do you remember?

### THE OLD WEST—BAD BART COMES TO TOWN

*Sesame Street* used the setting of the Old West frequently—usually to show us how our fears were unfounded. Here's a classic example.

*(A crowd is gathered in a saloon in the Old West. Clementine bursts in.)*

**Clementine:** Hey everybody, listen up! I got some real bad news.

**Barkeep:** That a fact? You seldom hear a discouraging word 'round here.

**Clementine:** Well, I got two discouraging words: *Bad Bart. (Everyone murmurs and shakes—they're worried)* He said he's gonna give somebody "what they deserve," and he'll be in here to give it when the cow moos four.

**Luke:** That's kinda unusual, ain't it? Folks usually ride into town at high noon, not when the cow moos four.

**Clementine:** Well, you know Bad Bart. A real individual. Likes to do things his own way.

*(They hear four train whistles and try to figure out if that means Bart is on his way. They agree that it isn't time. They then hear four dog whistles, and again think it*
might be time to see Bad Bart. Finally, the cow moos four times.)*

**Barkeep:** Is it okay to get scared and riled up?

**Clementine:** Yep. Help, help! Bad Bart's coming! Help, help! *(Hides under a table as Bad Bart enters)* Howdy, Bad. Lookin' pretty good. Been workin' out with weights, have yuh?

**Bad Bart:** Shut up. I'm here to give somebody what he deserves. *(Collective gasp)*

**Luke:** Who?

**Bad Bart:** The bartender. *(Moseys on over to the barkeep)* You remember the last time I was here?

**Barkeep:** Y-y-yessir?

**Bad Bart:** Remember I asked fer some sarsaparilla an' you didn't have it!

**Barkeep:** Uh-huh?

**Bad Bart:** Remember you rode to the next town to get some and *kept me waitin'*!

**Barkeep:** Yes.

**Bad Bart:** Good. Then you'll remember I fergot to pay yuh. *(Gives him coins)* There. I gave you what you deserve.

# the celebrities

Sesame Street has had hundreds of celebrity visitors over its thirty years, starting with **James Earl Jones** and **Burt Lancaster** in 1969 (they counted and said the alphabet with more feeling and nuance than any of us previously thought possible). Here's a tribute to some of *Sesame*'s famous celebrity guests, along with a few awards they should have received for their outstanding performances.

## THE HAPPY-FEET AWARD

To **Jim Carrey**, accepting for Steve Martin. Jim took over a bit that was originally written for Steve—a demonstration of "Sad Feet" and "Happy Feet." When Jim read it, he commented that "this sounds like a Steve Martin bit." The writers assured him it wasn't.

Danny DeVito

**psssst!!**

### secret fact:

When Burt Lancaster came on the show, one bit he taped required him to count while doing one-handed push-ups. According to Gerry Lesser, director of research for *Sesame Street* at the time, Lancaster was concentrating so intensely on his one-handed push-ups "he couldn't remember to count as he was doing them. We kept doing take after take."

## THE LET'S DO THE TIME WARP AGAIN AWARD

For **Susan Sarandon**'s *Rocky Horror Picture Show*-esque scene with The Count, they're standing outside a castle, it's raining, and they decide to knock on the castle door. The Count, of course, wants to knock again and again and again, even though it's clear that no one's home. **When Susan points this out, The Count informs her that he knows that there's no one home—it's his castle! He** just wanted to knock for the joy of counting.

**pssst!!**

**secret fact:** James Earl Jones, the first celebrity to appear on the show, was mentored at the American Theater Wing by Will Lee, who played Mr. Hooper.

The Now I Know My ABCs Award

(celebrities who have said or sung the alphabet)

Harry Belafonte
Mary Chapin Carpenter
Ray Charles
Bill Cosby
Ellen DeGeneres
**James Earl Jones**
Burt Lancaster
Shari Lewis and Lambchop
Susan Sarandon
Patrick Stewart

Susan Sarandon

Everything on *Sesame Street* has to appeal to children on their own level. We don't do anything that's only interesting to adults; it has to entertain on two levels if we're doing adult humor. That's why we use celebrities—because they help adults watch the show.

—Michael Loman, Executive Producer of *Sesame Street*

Rosie O'Donnell

> **There are friendly people in my neighborhood.**
> —Rosie O'Donnell on what she's learned from *Sesame Street*

## THE TEACH WHAT YOU KNOW AWARD

**Arthur Ashe** demonstrated "Up" by hitting a tennis ball into the air, and "Down" by being clobbered by a cascade of tennis balls.

**David Robinson** agreed to dribble as many times as he could while The Count counted. He ended up missing his dinner engagement.

**Joe Namath**—For his suave "Forward Pass/Backward Pass" demonstration.

**Bo Jackson** brought "Bo Knows" to the Street: "Bo knows letters," "Bo knows counting," "Bo knows up and down."

## MUPPETS AND THEIR CELEBRITY COUNTERPARTS

Could Meryl Sheep have been Meryl Streep's stunt double in *The River Wild*? Could Placido Flamingo take Placido Domingo's place in the middle of the Three Tenors? Could Polly Darton sing "Nine to Five" with the same feeling as Dolly Parton? Take a look and decide for yourself.

Meryl Sheep and **Meryl Streep**

Placido Flamingo and **Placido Domingo**

Polly Darton and **Dolly Parton**

Baa Baa Walters and **Barbara Walters**

Bennett Snerf and **Bennett Cerf**

Pat Playjacks and **Pat Sajak**

Ross Parrot and **Ross Perot**

Warren Wolf and **Warner Wolf**

Ronnie Trash and **Johnny Cash**

Placido Domingo

Polly Darton

### IT'S A BEAUTIFUL DAY IN THE NEIGHBORHOOD...

Fred Rogers once asked Big Bird to be on his show, and Spinney said he'd love to do it. Spinney then received a script for the episode that required him to *remove his costume* and talk about how Big Bird works. Spinney declined, explaining, "Fantasy is one of the wonderful things of childhood, and it only lasts a little while." Mr. Rogers understood, but explained that on his show, Big Bird could then only be seen in the Land of Make-Believe. In the end, Spinney did the show, but Big Bird stayed in the Land of Make Believe with King Friday and Lady Elaine Fairchild.

Meryl Sheep

**Phil Donahue**

I especially remember Maria. She helped me spell and pronounce Snuffleupagus.
—Phil Donahue

## THE BEFORE THEY WERE STARS AWARD

Most of the celebrities who appeared on *Sesame Street* were already famous. But a few well-known actors and personalities actually appeared on the show *before* they became well-known.

**Alan Arkin** (featured in *Edward Scissorhands* and *The In-Laws*): Was part of an early comedy duo, "Larry and Phyllis," who discussed educational concepts in a decidedly twisted vaudevillian manner.

**Paul Bendict** (the neighbor in *The Jeffersons* who always needed George to walk on his back): Wore a white coat and painted numbers on everything!

**Paul Bendict**

**Savion Glover** (dancer and choreographer of *Bring in Da Noise, Bring in Da Funk*): Was a main character on the Street who played Gina's close friend.

**Raul Julia** (known as Gomez Addams in the *Addams Family* movies, other major films, and on Broadway): Played Rafael for a brief time on the show.

**Charlotte Rae** (Mrs. Garrett from *The Facts of Life* and *Diff'rent Strokes*): Played Molly the mail carrier on the show.

### The "Just Do It" Award

BO

(some celebrity sports figures who have been on the show)

Arthur Ashe
The Double Dutch Jump Rope Dancers
Julius Erving
Peggy Fleming
Harlem Globetrotters
Roosevelt "Rosie" Grier
**Bo Jackson**
Joe Namath
Martina Navratilova
New York Giants
New York Knicks
New York Mets
Isiah Thomas
Dave Winfield

**John Goodman**

**Noah Wyle**

Being on *Sesame Street* was the crowning achievement of my career.
—Noah Wyle

Gene Siskel

Roger Ebert

On Sesame Street, being kind is a good thing—and so is expressing joy.
—Gene Siskel, on what he's learned from Sesame Street

Muppets are people, too.
—Roger Ebert, on what he's learned from Sesame Street

I hear more from people who see me on Sesame Street singing "Put Down the Duckie" than from almost any interview I do.
—Barbara Walters

Barbara Walters

David Robinson

141

James Taylor

**The Sing-Along Award**

A star in the making joined Paul Simon in "Me and Julio Down by the Schoolyard"— and made up an additional verse on the spot.

**FAMOUS ENTERTAINERS WHO HAVE PERFORMED ON *SESAME STREET*:**

Harry Belafonte
Tony Bennett
Rubén Bladés
Cab Calloway
Tracy Chapman
Ray Charles
Chubby Checker

**S** Has sponsored show more than: 150 times
Has stood for:
Sing, Sleigh, Sammy the Snake, Suitcase, Subway

Judy Collins
Bo Diddley
Gloria Estefan
Melissa Etheridge
José Feliciano
Fourteen Karat Soul
Four Tops

James Galway
Dizzy Gillespie
Crystal Gayle
Herbie Hancock
Lena Horne
Mahalia Jackson
Waylon Jennings

Ray Charles

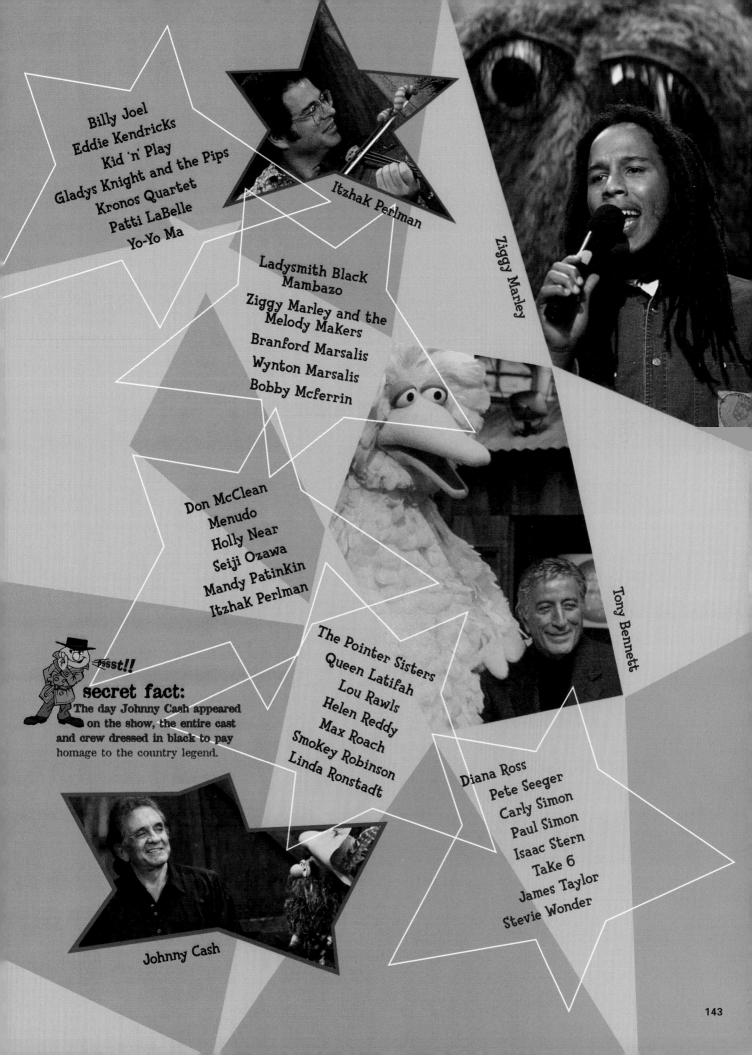

Billy Joel
Eddie Kendricks
Kid 'n' Play
Gladys Knight and the Pips
Kronos Quartet
Patti LaBelle
Yo-Yo Ma

Itzhak Perlman

Ziggy Marley

Ladysmith Black
Mambazo
Ziggy Marley and the
Melody Makers
Branford Marsalis
Wynton Marsalis
Bobby Mcferrin

Don McClean
Menudo
Holly Near
Seiji Ozawa
Mandy Patinkin
Itzhak Perlman

Tony Bennett

The Pointer Sisters
Queen Latifah
Lou Rawls
Helen Reddy
Max Roach
Smokey Robinson
Linda Ronstadt

pssst!!

**secret fact:**
The day Johnny Cash appeared
on the show, the entire cast
and crew dressed in black to pay
homage to the country legend.

Diana Ross
Pete Seeger
Carly Simon
Paul Simon
Isaac Stern
Take 6
James Taylor
Stevie Wonder

Johnny Cash

chapter four

# Sing—Sing a Song
## The Music and Poems
## of *Sesame Street*

Sing!
Sing a song
Sing out loud
Sing out strong
Sing of good things, not bad
Sing of happy, not sad!

Words and music by Joe Raposo
Copyright © 1971 Jonico Music, Inc. (BMI)

The songs and poems of *Sesame Street* aren't just for children, or for a certain moment in time. They are timeless classics, and for everyone. Joe Raposo, *Sesame Street*'s songwriter and musical director for eleven years (from 1969–1974 and again from 1983–1989), told his band that the songs were never written for children alone: "We're just dealing with a very short audience."

Many of *Sesame Street*'s songs have become classics in their own right. "Bein' Green" is a song about acceptance and loving who you are, a song that appeals to children, adults, and frogs alike. "Sing" touches a chord in everyone. Even adults still laugh at "C is for Cookie" and at Ernie's ode to his "Rubber Duckie."

Here are the songs and poems two generations of kids have grown up with.

Did You Know?

Sesame Street has won eight Grammys to date.

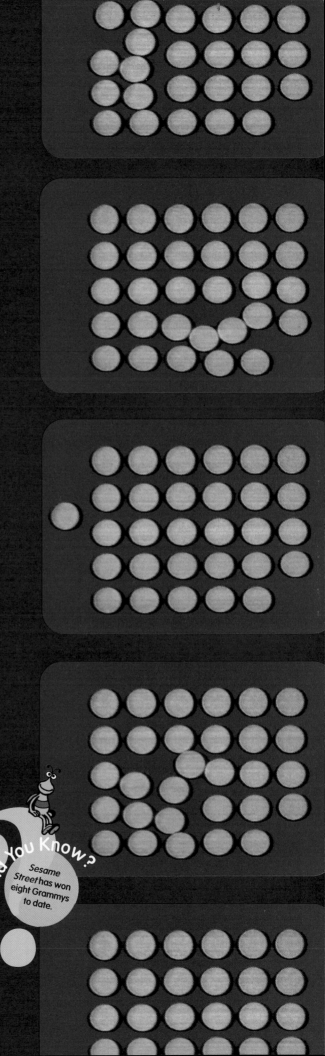

# SiNG

Words and music by Joe Raposo
Copyright © 1971 Jonico Music, Inc. (BMI)

la la do la-da
la-da la-do la-da-la
da-da la-do-la-da

Sing!
Sing a song
Sing out loud
Sing out strong
Sing of good things, not bad
Sing of happy, not sad

Sing!
Sing a song
Make it simple
To last your whole life long
Don't worry that it's not good enough
For anyone else to hear
Sing!
Sing a song

La la do la-da
la-da la-do la-da-la
da-da la-do-la-da

la la do la-da
la-da la-do la-da-la
da-da la-do-la-da

Sing!
Sing a song
Sing out loud
Sing out strong
Sing of good things, not bad
Sing of happy, not sad

Sing!
Sing a song
Make it simple
To last your whole life long
Don't worry that it's not good enough
For anyone else to hear
Sing!
Sing a song
La la do la-da
la-da la-do la-da-la
da-da la-do-la-da

**ᵖssst!!**

## secret facts:

✿ Danny Epstein, current musical coordinator of *Sesame Street*, remembers hearing "Sing" for the first time: "Joe called me and said he had just written this song. He gets to the bridge, and he starts going 'La, la, la-la-la, la, la, la, la-la-la, la-la la la-la-la-la,' and he asks me, 'What do you think?' I said, 'It sounds like you ran out of words.'"

✿ The Carpenters' remake of "Sing" became a Top 40 hit.

# BEIN' GREEN

Words and music by Joe Raposo
Copyright © 1970 Jonico Music, Inc. (BMI)

It's not that easy bein' green
Having to spend each day the color of the leaves

When I think it could be nicer
Bein' red, or yellow, or gold
Or something much more colorful like that
It's not easy bein' green

It seems you blend in with so many other ordinary things
And people tend to pass you over
'Cause you're not standing out like flashy sparkles on the water
Or stars in the sky

But green's the color of spring
And green can be cool and friendly-like,
And green can be big, like an ocean,
Or important like a mountain
Or tall like a tree
When green is all there is to be,
It could make you wonder why
But why wonder? Why wonder?
I am green, and it'll do fine
It's beautiful,
And I think it's what I want to be

**=pssst!!**

## secret facts:

✿ "Bein' Green" has been sung on the show by Kermit, Lena Horne, and Ray Charles.

✿ "Bein' Green" was on Frank Sinatra's album *The Man and His Music.*

✿ The lyrics to "Bein' Green" were published in a hardcover book by Western Publishing in 1979. It was illustrated by Etienne Delessert, the renowned illustrator of more than thirty adult and children's books.

# Would you like to buy an O?

Words and music by Joe Raposo
Copyright © 1973 Jonico Music, Inc. (BMi)

Would you like to buy an O
Round and neat?
A nearly perfect circle
Tidy and complete
You can sing a pretty song with it like so,
"Oh-oh-oh oh-oh oh"
(Isn't that catchy?)

Would ya like to buy an O?
Circular and sweet?
O looks just like a doughnut—
Really good enough to eat
It'll cost ya just a nickel
[Ernie: A nickel!]
Shhhh!
[Ernie (whispers): A nickel?]
Riiiiiight

So buy the O and take it home tonight
When you buy this O you get two sounds for the price of one
Ya get one sound that you can use for words like olive, ostrich, and ox
And for no extra money you get another sound for words like
Ocean, over, old, and opening.
So would you like to buy an O?
I'm opening the door
It's not often that I offer
Well, who could ask for more?
It'll cost you just a nickel
[Ernie: A nickel!]
Shhhh!
[Ernie (whispers): A nickel?]
Riiiiiight
So buy the O and take it home tonight
Don't ask any questions—
Just buy the O, and take it home tonight
You'll really love it!
Just buy the O, and take it home tonight

# Hey, Bud. See this U? We've had this U in my family for years....

—Lefty

Remember the slightly shifty salesman in the trenchcoat? He'd stop you on the street with an all-knowing "Psssst!", open his trenchcoat, and show you his wares.

### PSSST! OVER HERE! YOU WANNA BUY...

- ✿ An invisible ice-cream cone (Ernie bought it with an invisible nickel)
- ✿ A snowman (that for some strange reason got smaller and smaller)
- ✿ An O ("It only costs a nickel.")
- ✿ A U (it gets bent—so he tries to sell it as a V instead)

## do you remember?

*(Lefty and his accomplice, Fat Blue, are plotting to steal the Golden An)*

**Accomplice:** I want you to take this golden "An" in the tan van. Give it to Dan, who will take it to Fran. You understand?

*(Lefty repeats the plan to himself as a policeman comes up behind him)*

**Lefty:** Okay, I take the Golden An and put it in the tan truck. No wait...

**Policeman:** My name's Stan. I'm the man. You just got ten days in the can for stealing the Golden An. Let's go.

**Lefty:** Awwww—I shoulda ran!

### SAT: SESAME ACHIEVEMENT TEST

**SESAME STREET HAS NOT FEATURED A MUPPET COVER VERSION OF WHICH SONG?**

- A ○ "Good Morning Starshine"
- B ○ "Lucy in the Sky with Diamonds"
- C ○ "Ma Nah Ma Nah"
- D ○ "Muskrat Love"

*Answer: D. But only because the Captain and Tenille's version could never be surpassed.*

# PEOPLE IN YOUR NEIGHBORHOOD

**Words and music by Jeff Moss**
Copyright © 1970 Festival Attractions, Inc. (ASCAP)

"People in Your Neighborhood" was written to introduce children to different occupations through the working lives of their neighbors. It was used in Muppet inserts, with celebrity guests, and in films.

**pssst!!**
### secret fact:
When consumer advocate Ralph Nader appeared on the show, he sang "People in Your Neighborhood" with Bob, including the verse, "The consumer advocate's a person in your neighborhood." But Nader pointed out a grammatical error in the last stanza. He insisted that a line be changed from "the people *that* you meet each day" to "the people *whom* you meet each day." The musical director agreed to the change, but returned to the original lyrics afterward.

**N** Has sponsored show more than: 120 times

Has stood for:
Nine, Nail, Nancy, Nanny goat, Neighborhood, Naughty

Oh, who are the people in your neighborhood,
In your neighborhood,
In your neigh-bor-hood?
Oh, who are the people in your neighborhood,
The people that you meet each day?

Oh, the postman always brings the mail,
Through rain or snow or sleet or hail.
He'll work and work the whole day through
To get your letters safe to you.
'Cause the postman is a person in your neighborhood
In your neighborhood,
He's in your neigh-bor-hood!
A postman is a person in your neighborhood,
A person that you meet each day.

Oh, a fireman is brave it's said.
His engine is a shiny red.
If there's a fire anywhere about,
Well, he'll be sure to put it out.

Oh, a fireman is a person in your neighborhood,
In your neighborhood,
In your neighborhood,

And the postman is a person in your neighborhood,
They're the people that you meet
When you're walking down the street
They're the people that you meet each day!

# one of

Words by Jon Stone
Music by Joe Raposo
Copyright © 1970 Instructional Children's Music, Inc. (ASCAP)

One of these things
Is not like the others.
One of these things
Just doesn't belong.
Can you tell which thing
Is not like the others
By the time I finish my song?

Did you guess which thing
Is not like the others?
Did you guess real hard
With all of your might?
If you guessed *this* thing
Is not like the others,
Then you're absolutely right!

# these

# things

**≈pssst!!**

## secret fact:
John-John, one of *Sesame Street*'s regular "real kid" visitors, once pretended to be Bob and sang "One of These Things" while Bob pretended to be John-John and answered the questions.

*ssssst!!*

## secret facts:

☆ The now-famous Rubber Duckie solo that punctuates the song was originally squeaked by Jeff Moss when the song was recorded for the first *Sesame Street* album.

☆ According to Danny Epstein, musical coordinator for *Sesame Street*, when the cast played this song with the Boston Pops (Big Bird conducted), the musicians were not allowed to squeeze rubber duckies in addition to playing their own instruments unless they were paid extra. Apparently, a rubber duckie was considered to be a second instrument, and each musician was supposed to receive additional pay if they played a second instrument. When it came time for the actual performance, only the percussion players squeaked the ducks. It was determined that the rubber duck was to be considered a percussion instrument.

☆ During the performance with the Boston Pops, Will Lee (Mr. Hooper) was to play a triangle. But he couldn't read sheet music, so he didn't know when his cues were. After trying several solutions, someone decided to tie a rope to Lee's leg. Offstage, Danny Epstein, the current musical coordinator, and Joe Raposo tugged the rope and flashed a signal flashlight whenever Lee was supposed to play.

☆ In 1996, "Rubber Duckie" was a huge hit in Germany (the German Ernie sang it in German). A CD with five different versions of the song, including a "dance remix" sold 1.8 million copies.

Words and music by Jeff Moss
Sung by: Jim Henson as Ernie.
Copyright © 1970 Festival Attractions, Inc. (ASCAP)

# Rubber Duckie

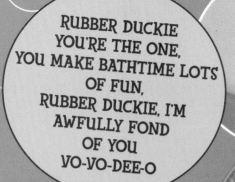

RUBBER DUCKIE
YOU'RE THE ONE,
YOU MAKE BATHTIME LOTS
OF FUN,
RUBBER DUCKIE, I'M
AWFULLY FOND
OF YOU
VO-VO-DEE-O

RUBBER DUCKIE,
JOY OF JOYS,
WHEN I SQUEEZE YOU,
YOU MAKE NOISE,
RUBBER DUCKIE YOU'RE
MY VERY BEST FRIEND
IT'S TRUE.

OH,
EVERY DAY
WHEN I, MAKE MY
WAY TO THE TUBBY
I FIND A LITTLE FELLOW
WHO'S CUTE AND
YELLOW AND CHUBBY!
RUB-A-DUB-
DUB-BY!

RUBBER DUCKIE
YOU'RE SO FINE,
AND I'M LUCKY THAT
YOU'RE MINE
RUBBER DUCKIE, I'D LOVE A
WHOLE POND OF, RUBBER
DUCKIE, I'M AWFULLY
FOND OF YOU!

OH,
EVERY DAY
WHEN I, MAKE MY
WAY TO THE TUBBY
I FIND A LITTLE FELLOW
WHO'S CUTE AND
YELLOW AND CHUBBY!
RUB-A-DUB-
DUB-BY!

RUBBER DUCKIE
YOU'RE SO FINE,
AND I'M LUCKY THAT
YOU'RE MINE
RUBBER DUCKIE
I'M AWFULLY FOND
OF YOU!

# MONSTER IN THE MIRROR

Words by Norman Stiles
Music by Christopher Cerf
Copyright © 1990 Splotched Animal Music (BMI)/Sesame Street, Inc. (ASCAP)

Saw a monster in the mirror when I woke up today—
A monster in my mirror but I did not run away.
I did not shed a tear or hide beneath my bed
Though the monster looked at me and this is what he said—

He said, "Wubba wubba wubba wubba woo woo woo,
Wubba wubba wubba and a doodly do."
He sang, "Wubba wubba wubba," so I sang it too!
No do not wubba me or I will wubba you!
Do not wubba me or I will wubba you.

(Told the) monster in the mirror, "No, I am not scared."
Then I smiled at him and thanked him for the song that we had shared
Well, the monster thanked me too he smiled right back and then
The monster in the mirror sang his song again—

He sang, "Wubba wubba wubba wubba woo woo woo,
Wubba wubba wubba and a doodly do."
He went, "Wubba wubba wubba," and I sang along!
Yes, wubba wubba wubba is a monster song—
Wubba wubba wubba is a monster song

(If your) mirror has a monster in it do not shout
This kind of situation does not call for freaking out
And do nothing that you would not like to see him do
'Cause that monster in the mirror he just might be you!

Singing, "Wubba wubba wubba wubba woo woo woo,
Wubba wubba wubba and a doodly do."
He went, "Wubba wubba wubba" you can join in, too!"
Yes, if you wubba me then I will wubba you!
If you wubba me then I will wubba you!

pssst!!

## secret fact:
On the show, the songs "Monster in the Mirror" and "Put Down the Duckie" featured not only Grover and Ernie, respectively, but also dozens of celebrity guests who sang along (celebrities like Candice Bergen, Paul Simon, Jeremy Irons, Danny DeVito, The Simpsons, Ray Charles, and many more). The producers and directors on the show did not book all of these celebrities on one day to record their parts. Instead, they recorded them throughout the season. Each time a celebrity came on the show the producers taped a verse with that celebrity. At the end of the season, producers spliced the celebrity verses into one long song.

# C is for Cookie

Words and music by Joe Raposo
Copyright © 1973 Jonico Music, Inc. (BMI)

Now, what starts with the letter C?
    Cookie starts with C!
Let's think of other things that start with C...
    Ahhh, who cares about the other things!

C is for Cookie, that's good enough for me.
    C is for Cookie, that's good enough for me.
C is for Cookie, that's good enough for me.
    Oh, Cookie, Cookie, Cookie, starts with C.


C is for Cookie, that's good enough for me.
    C is for Cookie, that's good enough for me.
        C is for Cookie, that's good enough for me.
    Oh, Cookie, Cookie, Cookie, starts with C.

sssst!!
secret facts:
✿ Candice Bergen sang this song on *Sesame Street*.
✿ C is for cavity, too—so brush your teeth after
eating cookies!

C Has
sponsored show more
than: 150 times
Has stood for:
Cake, Canary, Cap,
Carrot, Cat, Cookie,
Cowboy

I love pigeons. I love how they walk, and I've created a really cool dance called "Doin' the Pigeon."
—Bert

# Doin' the Pigeon —coo coo!

Words and music by Joe Raposo
Copyright © 1973 Wizzybus Music, Inc. (BMI)

Every time I feel alone and slightly blue
That's when I begin to think that's what I'd like to start to do
And though it may not be the kind of thing that's quite your
 cup of tea
I recommend you pay attention to the little dance you're
 gonna see!

Next to Ernie, oatmeal, and marching band music, pigeons are what make Bert most happy. He so admires the way they move, the way they coo, the way they live that he's invented a dance to capture the joy that pigeons make him feel. And now, with this handy guide, we can all learn how to do it, too.

(Lift leg)
Doin'—the coo coo!
(Move leg and head back and forth once, like a pigeon)
Pigeon!
[Are you doin' it?]
(Lift leg)
Doin'—the coo coo!
(Move leg and head back and forth once, like a pigeon)
Pigeon!
[Faster!]

Dancing a little smidgeon of the
Kind of ballet
Sweeps me away

(Lift leg)
Doin'—the coo coo!
(Move leg and head back and forth once, like a pigeon)
Pigeon!
[There you go!]

(Lift leg)
Doin'—the coo coo!
(Move leg and head back and forth once, like a pigeon)
Pigeon!
[Isn't this terrific?]

People may smile but I don't mind
They'll never understand the kind of fun I find

(Lift leg)
Doin'—the coo coo!
(Move leg and head back and forth once, like a pigeon)
Pigeon!
[We're really cooin' now!]

(Lift leg)
Doin'—the coo coo!
(Move leg and head back and forth once, like a pigeon)
Pigeon!
[Who says I'm square?]

Doin' the pigeon every day!

# FLIP-BOOK!

(instructions on back)

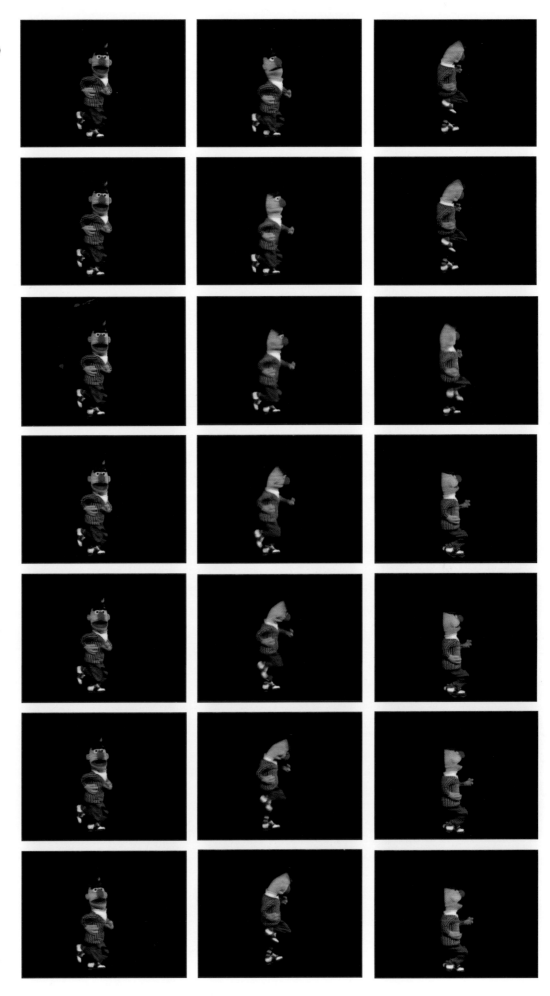

| 15 | 8 | 1 |
| 16 | 9 | 2 |
| 17 | 10 | 3 |
| 18 | 11 | 4 |
| 19 | 12 | 5 |
| 20 | 13 | 6 |
| 21 | 14 | 7 |

## DOIN' THE PIGEON FLIP-BOOK INSTRUCTIONS:

**1.** Cut along dotted lines.

**2.** Stack flip-book pages picture-side up from 1 to 48, with #1 on top.

**3.** Securely clamp flip-book pages together along left-hand side using a binder clip or clothes pin.

**4.** Riffle pages along right-hand side with your thumb and watch Bert dance!

| 43 | 36 | 29 | 22 |
| 44 | 37 | 30 | 23 |
| 45 | 38 | 31 | 24 |
| 46 | 39 | 32 | 25 |
| 47 | 40 | 33 | 26 |
| 48 | 41 | 34 | 27 |
| 49 | 42 | 35 | 28 |

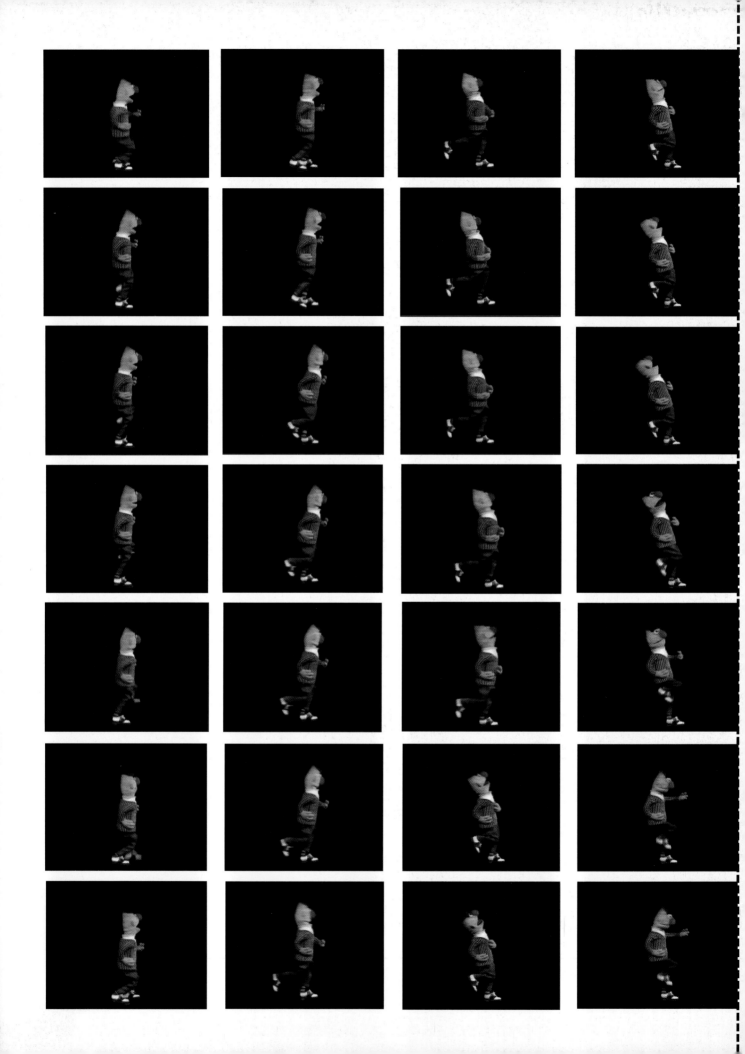

"Bert *is* the Pigeon."
—Frank Oz

I love galoshes
they give me a thrill
cold mashed potatoes
I can't get my fill
I go for plumbing
And I always will
I'm square
I'm square
—Bert, "I'm Square"

What is this? A hundred glamorous pictures of pigeons, and no one wants to look at them!
—Bert

CONTRARY TO POPULAR BELIEF, BERT IS NOT PIGEON-TOED.

# The Poetry of Sesame Street

The rhythm and rhyme of *Sesame Street* is unparalleled. The beat on the Street is the original spoken word—it was the hip before hop, has more beats than the beatniks, and is freer than any free verse you've ever heard. It's also hilarious. Here's some of *Sesame Street*'s classic verse. Read it aloud in a coffeehouse near you.

## THE EXTRA-SMOOTH POETRY OF ROOSEVELT FRANKLIN

RHYME TIME, RHYME TIME! EVERYBODY READY FOR RHYME TIME?

—Roosevelt Franklin

Roosevelt Franklin was many things—a student and lover of the blues—but mostly, he was a budding young poet who could rhyme words faster than you could think of 'em. Here are some of his greatest works, and a few from his fellow students at Roosevelt Franklin Elementary School.

## Same Sound Brown

by Roosevelt Franklin

Same Sound Brown was a rhymin' man
He would rhyme words faster than I bet you can
See, if you said, "Moose,"
Brown would say "Juice."
If you say "Moose Juice,"
Brown would say, "Loose Goose."
If you said, "Juicy Loose Goose,"
Brown would say, "Moosey Goose Juice."

# Tryin'

by Hard Head Henry Harris

I tried this pair of roller skates
I kept on falling down.
I looked so simple tryin' to skate—
I looked just like a clown.

But now listen, I kept on tryin'
tryin and tryin' and tryin'.
And in a little while, my feet was flyin'!
Now I can skate straight—
And I can skate curvy—

And now I'm ready for
the roller derby!

# Still Tryin'

by Baby Bree Boo Bop a Doo

Over in the swimmin' pool nine weeks ago
I didn't even have the nerve to
stick in my little toe.
Swimmin' teacher talkin' 'bout,
"Go ahead and try!"
I climbed up on a bench and I
looked him in the eye
And said, "Okay, man, but let me
tell you this, too—
If sumpin' happens to me, I'm comin'
lookin' for you!"

So I made up my mind to keep on tryin'
And listen to this-if I'm lyin', I'm flyin'!
I got to kickin' and strokin' 'til now
I got the notion,
I can backstroke and butterfly clear
across the ocean!

# Tryin' Again

by Smart Tina

I tried to grow these tomato seeds
And all I saw was a bunch of weeds.
I pulled up the weeds on out the way
and watched the ground for half a day!

The more I waited, the madder I got,
Sittin' out there with the sun all hot.
But I saw somethin' a few days later—
A little bitty plant, with no tomato!

And I kept waitin', watchin' it grow.
Months went by, and don't you know,
I didn't mind that long ol' wait—
'Cause I got tomato on
my plate!

# I AM—SOMEBODY

by the Reverend Jesse R. Jackson and a whole bunch of kids

It was 1971. Nixon was in the midst of Watergate, *All in the Family* was the new hit TV show, and Jesse Jackson came on *Sesame Street*. Jesse sat on the stoop of 123 Sesame Street, and a large group of children filled the street around him. They sat on the ground, on benches, and on fire escapes. And then Jesse led them in a poem. It was one of the more powerful moments that ever happened on the show.

So read this poem out loud, like Jesse and the kids did. Shout it out the window. Scream it from your car. And remember, you heard it first on *Sesame Street*.

I AM
SOMEBODY
I AM
SOMEBODY
I MAY BE POOR
BUT I AM
SOMEBODY
I MAY BE YOUNG
BUT I AM
SOMEBODY
I MAY BE ON WELFARE
BUT I AM
SOMEBODY
I MAY BE SMALL
BUT I AM
SOMEBODY
I MAY MAKE A MISTAKE
BUT I AM
SOMEBODY
MY CLOTHES ARE DIFFERENT
MY FACE IS DIFFERENT
MY HAIR IS DIFFERENT
BUT I AM
SOMEBODY
I AM BLACK
BROWN
WHITE
I SPEAK A DIFFERENT LANGUAGE
BUT I MUST BE RESPECTED
PROTECTED
NEVER REJECTED
I AM
GOD'S CHILD
I AM
SOMEBODY

**JESSE: GIVE YOURSELF A HAND.**

# Fat Cat

Poem by Joe Raposo

Fat
Cat
Sat
Hat

A fat cat sat on a hat, saw a
rat on mat,
got a bat, had a chat with a gnat
that he'd pat
in a vat that was flat, oh yeah!

Small
Ball
Tall
Wall

See the small ball on the tall wall,
see it fall in a hall see it crawl
give its all and call "Hi y'all!"
see it stall, wear a shawl, oh yeah!

Red
Head
Fed
Bread

See the red head bein' fed bread
on his sled made of lead,
as he's sped to be wed but he
fled instead out ahead up to Ted
and in bed and he said:

Red   Head   Fed   Bread
Small   Ball   Tall   Wall
Fat   Cat   Sat   Hat
And that's that!

**SCAT!**

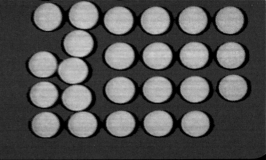

## chapter five

# "Psst! Hey Buddy!"
## Behind the Scenes
## on *Sesame Street*

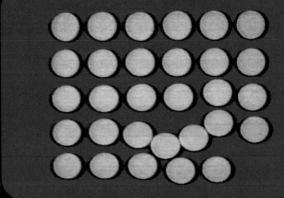

"There's a wonderful actor whom
the whole world will never get
to see under
Big Bird's costume.
Caroll Spinney, the actor,
never gets the credit—
it's alway Big Bird."

—Joey Mazzarino, Muppeteer and writer

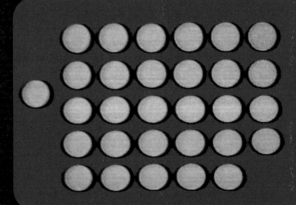

What really goes into the making of *Sesame Street* ? How
do the writers, producers, and creators make the show
every week? Where do they get their ideas? Who's behind
(or inside) the show's different Muppets, and how do they
bring those characters to life? How do the Muppets work—
especially the big ones like Big Bird or Snuffleupagus?
Where do Big Bird's feathers come from? What's really
inside Oscar's can?

   For all those who want to know how it feels to be part of
a cultural phenomenon, and for those who want to hear the
actors speak about what it's like, you've come to the right
place. If you've ever pondered the back roads and alleys of
the Street, this is the chapter you've been waiting for.

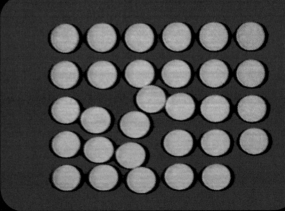

# THE MAKING OF A MUPPET

THE UNHERALDED HEROES OF THE SHOW ARE THE PUPPET BUILDERS.
—Caroll Spinney

The Muppets may look bright and new, but they have been around for quite a while. Jim Henson started making "Muppets" (a combination of the words "marionette" and "puppet") in the 1950s; their construction follows a puppet tradition that goes back for hundreds of years. "You can go all the way to Indonesia and find puppets that are made in a similar way," says Ed Christie, the *Sesame Street* Muppet art director. What Muppet builders introduced was the use of soft materials and synthetics, such as foam rubber.

Muppet builders are generally designers with backgrounds in sewing, pattern making, and sculpting. Each Muppet is made of the same basic raw materials—foam rubber, fur fabrics, and adhesives—raw materials they've been using since the early days. "There's an expression here, 'There are only so many Crayolas in the box.' We work with what we've got. These materials work the best," explains Christie.

## HOW TO MAKE A MUPPET, THE ABRIDGED VERSION:

1. Someone—a writer, producer, director, Muppeteer, or layperson—comes up with an idea for a new Muppet character and presents it to Ed Christie, the Muppet art director.

2. Christie draws initial sketches for the character based on the concepts he is given. He then gets feedback on the designs from the writers, directors, and Muppeteers, and narrows the selection down to one final design. He turns this design into a finished drawing.

3. Once the finished drawing is approved, Muppet builders pattern and sculpt the raw materials into a working puppet, or, as Christie terms it, a "moving sculpture." They then "dress" the raw foam character with fake furs, fabrics, and hemispheres for eyes and noses, as well as any other Muppet features that might be included (antennae, nose, horns, strange appendages, and so on).

4. If the puppet utilizes any mechanisms (for example, moving eyebrows, like Bert and Oscar; moving eyelids, like Big Bird; or remote-controlled motorized eyes, like Alice Snuffleupagus), engineers add them. And voilà! A Muppet comes to life—as long as there's a very talented hand inside it.

## THE MANY FACES OF THE MUPPETS: HOW THEY DO IT

### THE MAGIC TRIANGLE

✣ Each Muppet's face is designed using "the magic triangle," a formula for the relationship between the eyes and the nose that Jim Henson invented. It's still the anchor to the Muppet look. And it's still a secret!

✣ Muppet designers use different sized pupils depending upon how young or mature they want the Muppet to look. The smaller the pupil, the older the Muppet looks; the larger the pupil, the younger the Muppet looks.

**pssst!!**

**secret fact:**
Zoe's nose is actually made from a plastic grape covered in fleece.

### JEEPERS, CREEPERS—WHERE'D YOU GET THOSE PEEPERS?

✣ For years Muppet builders have used a toy called "Wacky Stacks" as a source for their Muppets' eyes. "Wacky Stacks" were a short-lived toy in the 1970s that worked sort of like a Russian nesting doll: a ball inside of a ball inside of a ball inside of a ball. Legend has it that Jim Henson bought out the entire inventory of "Wacky Stacks" when the company went under, and that inventory has been supplying Muppet eyes ever since.

### IS THAT A MARTIAN ON YOUR HEAD?

✣ Legend has it that *Sesame Street*'s famous Martians were originally made from chenille hats with fringes, hats that were apparently inspired by Elizabeth Taylor's headdress in the movie *Cleopatra*. The Martians are actually the hats turned upside down.

According to Nat Monjoy, *Sesame Street* props director, the most difficult prop his team ever had to create was a working giant telephone for Mr. Snuffleupagus.

# How the Muppets Work

Muppeteers don't usually memorize their lines. They work from a script that is taped to the monitor they're using, and a wall (or simply a high camera angle) is used to keep them out of the shot.

Jim Henson's style of lip synch is one of the things that has made his puppetry unique. Jerry Nelson (who plays The Count, Herry Monster, and many others) explained that the trick is to move the Muppet as if you're pushing the sounds out of your palm. In other words, don't just open and close the thumb and fingers. Among other things, Jim taught his Muppeteers how to use their hand and wrist movements to make the Muppet seem more alive.

## THE ANATOMY OF A BIRD

Caroll's right hand fits up into Big Bird's head and works the mouth and eyes. His left hand works Big Bird's left and right arms, and is the arm that can actually pick up things and perform actions. The right arm works like a marionette's, and is attached with an invisible wire to a ring in Big Bird's head, so whenever Caroll chooses he can make the right arm move with a bit of coordination. Okay, a *lot* of coordination.

Caroll has a microphone and a monitor inside the puppet that allows him to see what he's doing and who he's looking at. (His view is the same view the kids see at home).

Rod Muppets (like Kermit, Grover, and Bert) are worked by one Muppeteer, with the Muppeteer's right hand in the Muppet's mouth and the left hand working the rods, which are attached to the Muppet's hands or feet.

Two-handed Muppets (like Ernie, The Count, and Cookie Monster) take two Muppeteers to manipulate. They are "worn" by the Muppeteer who does the voice: the Muppet goes over his or her head, with the right hand in the Muppet's mouth and the left in the Muppet's left hand. The second Muppeteer puts his right hand into the Muppet's right hand. This is the hand that handles most of the props (cookies, rubber duckies, letters) and performs most of the action.

All of the Muppeteers usually work from the ground, either lying, sitting, or crouching down. The Muppeteers are usually propped up on a rolling cushion that allows them to move in and out of frame easily.

The Muppeteer does not look up at the Muppet or the other people in the scene, but rather watches a monitor displaying the same scene the viewer sees at home. The monitor allows the Muppeteer both to know where he is and to feel as if he is slightly removed from the Muppet, allowing the Muppet to have a life of its own. Since the eyes of most Muppets don't move, it's always important to be aware of where the "eyes" are focused.

## WHERE DID YOU GET THOSE BEAUTIFUL FEATHERS?

Although he was originally envisioned as a giant canary, Big Bird's costume is actually made with turkey feathers. The Jim Henson Company uses feathers that are purchased from a feather company here in the United States, then sends the feathers overseas to China so that the spine of each can be cut in half to make them less stiff, more supple.

The stripped feathers are sent back to the feather company, where they're bleached and cleaned. They are then dyed in two shades of yellow. The tips are dyed a bright yellow, and the downy part closest to the body is dyed a deeper, more golden yellow.

At the Muppet Workshop, builders separate the feathers into different "grades"—A, B, C, D, and E. Each feather must be about eight to nine inches long and in perfect shape, with no holes or turkey bite marks. Only A, B, and C feathers are used for the main costume. Most D and E feathers are thrown away.

Builders then hot glue the feathers onto the base of the Big Bird costume (Note: Caroll Spinney is *not* in the costume at this point in the process).

Every so often, Big Bird comes in to the Muppet Workshop for a makeover. At the end of each day of shooting, Muppet repair experts work to fix or replace feathers that have broken or fallen off. At the end of each season, Big Bird is given a complete overhaul, and all broken or stripped feathers are replaced. Approximately every five years the costume is completely stripped and re-feathered because the studio lights fade the color, making Big Bird appear slightly greenish.

> I think the simplest characters, like Bert or Ernie, are the most difficult to build. To get the simplicity to a point where the abstraction works is difficult. You can put eyes on a mop and call it a puppet, but to sculpt, and tweak, and make sure that the mouth works, get the mask right, the eyes right, is a lot of work.... It's like doing minimalist abstract sculpture or painting— the shapes are basic, so they need a carefully balanced application in order to be accepted as living characters.
>
> —Ed Christie, Muppet art director

**pssst!!**

### secret fact:
Most Muppets are replaced every five years. Cookie, Bert, Ernie, Grover, and Kermit are replaced every ten to twelve years.

## SAT: SESAME ACHIEVEMENT TEST (ANATOMY SECTION)

***SESAME STREET* USES APPROXIMATELY \_\_\_\_ PAIRS OF EYES AND \_\_\_\_ NOSES PER SEASON.**

A ● 100/50
B ● 1,000/5,000
C ● 219/180
D ● 2,190/1,800

*Answer: C. That's a lot of plastic surgery.*

**ACCORDING TO JANE HENSON, THE WORD "MUPPET" COMES FROM A COMBINATION OF:**

A ● mop and puppet
B ● manipulate and puppet
C ● marionette and puppet
D ● my and puppet
E ● mud and puppy

*Answer: C. Because the rods Muppets use are like those used in marionettes.*

**IT TAKES APPROXIMATELY \_\_\_\_ FEATHERS TO MAKE A BIG BIRD COSTUME.**

A ● 1,000
B ● 2,000
C ● 3,000
D ● 4,000

*Answer: D. But that's not enough to make even one down comforter.*

**BIG BIRD'S COSTUME WEIGHS AS MUCH AS_____.**

A ● 4 lbs. of birdseed
B ● 30 lbs. of birdseed
C ● 100 lbs. of birdseed
D ● 75 lbs. of birdseed

*Answer: A. But that's according to Caroll.*

# The World of Sesame Street

Just in case you happen to find yourself on *Sesame Street*, here's a map to help you get around.

**Maria and Luis' Fix-It Shop
(next to Hooper's Store)**
"You break 'em, we take 'em."
The place to bring your
toaster when it just won't
toast anymore.

**Bob's Apartment
(above Hooper's Store)**
Where Bob lives, and
sings in the shower.

FIX-IT SHOP

**The Arbor Area**
Home to the ever-popular tire swing.

**Hooper's Store (around the bend from 123)**
Where you can get a yo-yo, a harmonica, a sand bucket, or two fried eggs with ham, toast, and coffee, all for just $1.80.

**Ernie and Bert (basement of 123)**
Where the ducks are rubber, the
pigeons dance, and bedtime is
never as quiet as it should be.

**The Robinsons
(first floor of 123)**
Where Gordon, Susan,
and Miles live, and milk
and cookies abound.

**The Rodriguezes
(second floor of 123)**
Where Maria, Luis, and
Gabriela live, and
the door is always *abierto*.

NO
PARKING

123

**Oscar's Trash Can
(in front of 123)—**
Where the Grouch is at his grouchiest.
What are you hangin' around for?
A tour? Now scram!

**Big Bird's Nest
(around the corner from 123)**
Where Bird nests, reads his
poems, and snores
up a storm.

SESAME STREET

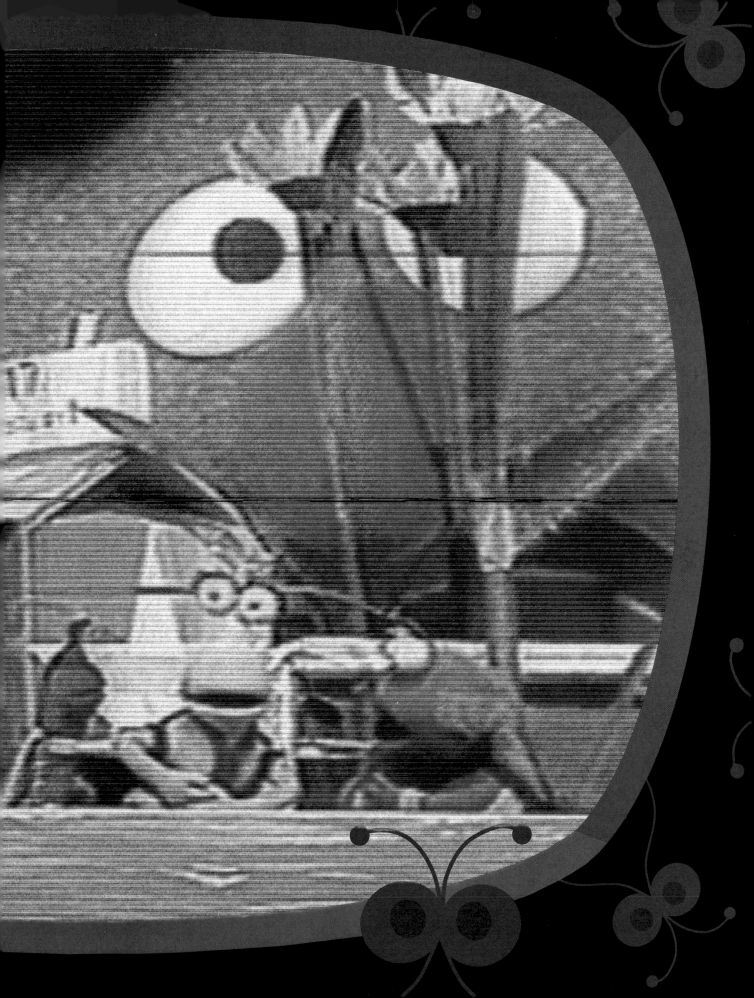

# AROUND THE WORLD

**LEFT:** *Rechov Sumsum/Shara'a Simsim*, the groundbreaking Israeli/Palestinian co-production of *Sesame Street,* premiered in 1998, and aims to teach mutual respect to preschool children living in Israel and the Palestinian Territories. Shown here are: Karim, a friendly Palestinian rooster who is proud of his plumage and his punctuality; Moishe Oofnik, the resident Israeli grouch, who like his American uncle Oscar the Grouch, delights in trash; Dafi, a purple, pigtailed monster whose enthusiasm and curiosity help her to learn new Arabic words from her new friend Haneen; and Haneen an orange monster who delights in learning Hebrew words.

**RIGHT:** In China, Hu Hu Zhu is an ageless, furry pig who is quite proud of his blue fur. He's also very proud of the long line of blue pigs from whom he is descended. Xiao Mei Zi ("Little Plum") is a bright red monster who is curious and level-headed. She also snores very loudly! *Zhima Jie,* the Chinese co-production of *Sesame Street* was launched in 1998 on Shanghai Television.

# WITH SESAME STREET

Did you know that *Sesame Street* has been broadcast in more than 140 countries around the world? Well, it's true. Some countries air the original American show, while other countries create new versions in their own languages.

## CHANNEL-SURFING AROUND THE WORLD

If you happen to be abroad and CNN International isn't what you're looking for, here's what *Sesame Street* has been called in other nations. You may not see the big yellow bird, but you will always enjoy great humor, great writing, and great puppets.

*Les Amis de Sesame*—France
*Barrio Sésamo*—Spain
*Iftah Ya Simsim*—Kuwait
*Plaza Sesamo*—Mexico
*Rechov Sumsum*—Israel
*Shara'a Sumsum*—Palestine Territories
*Rua Sésamo*—Portugal
*Sesam Stasjon*—Norway
*Sesame Park*—Canada
*Sesamstraat*—Holland
*Sesamstrasse*—Germany
*Susam Sokagi*—Turkey
*Ulica Sezamkowa*—Poland
*Ulitsa Sezam*—Russia
*Zhima Jie*—China
*Taman Sesame*—Malaysia
*Boneka Sesame*—Indonesia
*Sesam Opnist Pú*—Iceland
*Sezamé Otevri Se*—Czech Republic
*Svenska Sesam*—Sweden
*Seesamtie*—Finland

✿ Germany's grouchy character on *Sesamstrasse* is called Rumpel. He hates rain when others love it, but loves rain when others complain about it. *Sesamstrasse* was the first coproduction of *Sesame Street* outside the United States, and celebrates its twenty-fifth anniversary in 1998.

✿ Kuwait's *Iftah Ya Simsim*'s cast includes a tailor named Shaker and a street vendor, Abud-Allah, who sells books and other objects.

✿ Mexico's *Plaza Sesamo* features Abelardo Montoya in the Big Bird role. He's a seven-foot-tall green, yellow, and red parrot.

✿ Norway's *Sesam Stasjon* takes place in and around a train station.

✿ Canada's *Sesame Park* stars Basil, a lovable, lumbering polar bear and his French-Canadian otter pal, Louis.

LEFT: In Russia, the launch of *Ulitsa Sezam* in 1996 was a landmark achievement. Shown here (from left to right) are Kubik, a hand puppet who is inventive, sensible, and often caught up in his own thoughts; Zeliboba, a full-body puppet who wears a variety of tasteless ties; and Businka, a hand puppet, who is smart, happy, and happens to have a great hairdo.

Name that character: What the main players are called in other countries

| ENGLISH | ERNIE | BERT | COOKIE | KERMIT | GROVER |
|---|---|---|---|---|---|
| **Kuwait** | Anees | Bader | Ka'aki | Kamel | Gargoor |
| **Spain** | Epi | Blas | Triqui | Gustavo | Coco |
| **Mexico** | Enrique | Beto | Lucas | La Rana Rene | Archibaldo |
| **Norway** | Erling | Bernt | Kakemonsteret | Kermit | Gunnar |
| **Israel** | Arik | Bentz | Oogie | Kermit | Kruvi |
| **Sweden** | Ernie | Bert | Kakmonstret | Kermit | Greven |
| **Turkey** | Edi | Büdü | Kurabite Canavari | Kurbagacik | Açikgoz |
| **Russia** | Yenik | Vlas | Korzhik | Kermit | Grover |
| **Denmark** | Erik | Bent | Kage Monster | Kermit | Guffer |

**Did You Know?**
More than 120 million children have seen *Sesame Street* all around the world, making it (and CTW) the largest single teacher of young children on the planet.

Fran Brill as Prairie Dawn

Kevin Clash as Elmo

Frank Oz as Bert

Fran Brill as Zoe

# the muppeteers

**Jim Henson:** (1936–1990) Ernie, Kermit the Frog, Guy Smiley, MaNah MaNah, Captain Vegetable, Sinister Sam, Papa Twiddlebug, various Anything Muppets, various Martians (Note: Since 1991 Ernie and Kermit have been performed by Steve Whitmire.)

**Frank Oz:** Bert, Cookie Monster, Grover, Prince Charming, Harvey Kneeslapper, Professor Hastings, Mama Twiddlebug, The Salesman, various Anything Muppets, various Martians

**Jerry Nelson:** Herry Monster, Count von Count, Mr. Snuffleupagus (from 1971 to 1977), The Amazing Mumford, Biff the Hardhat, Fred the Wonder Horse,

Simon Soundman, Sherlock Hemlock, Fat Blue, Two-Headed Monster, Brother Twiddlebug, Herbert Birdsfoot, various Anything Muppets, various Martians

**Caroll Spinney:** Big Bird, Oscar the Grouch, Bruno the Trashman

**Fran Brill:** Prairie Dawn, Little Bird, Zoe, Countess Dahling von Dahling, Polly Darton, Baa Baa Walters, Wanda Cousteau, various Anything Muppets

**Martin Robinson:** Mr. Snuffleupagus (1980–present), Telly Monster, Buster the Horse, Slimey the Worm, various Anything Muppets, various Martians

**Kevin Clash:** Elmo, Hoots the Owl, Baby Natasha, Benny, Kingston Livingston II, various Anything Muppets

**Richard Hunt:** (1951–1992) Mr. Snuffleupagus (from 1977 to 1980), Forgetful Jones, Don Music, Gladys the Cow, Sully, Two-Headed Monster, Sonny Friendly, Placido Flamingo, Captain Vegetable, various Anything Muppets, various Martians

Jerry Nelson as Herry Monster

Frank Oz as Grover

Jim Henson as Ernie

Frank Oz as Cookie Monster

Caroll Spinney as Big Bird

**David Rudman:** Davey Monkey, Sonny Friendly, Humphrey, Baby Bear, various Anything Muppets

**Joey Mazzarino:** Joey Monkey, Colambo, Stinky the Stinkweed, various Anything Muppets

**Camille Kampouris:** Meryl Sheep, Goldilocks, Miss Muffet, Countess Von Backwards

**Pam Arciero:** Grungetta, various Anything Muppets

**Carmen Osbahr:** Rosita, various Anything Muppets

**Judy Sladky:** Alice Snuffleupagus, various Anything Muppets

**Bruce Connelly:** Barkley

**Matt Robinson:** Roosevelt Franklin (voice only)

Jim Henson as Kermit the Frog

Jerry Nelson as Count von Count

Caroll Spinney as Oscar the Grouch

# Jim Henson

*Working as I do with the movement of puppet creatures, I'm always struck by the feebleness of our efforts to achieve naturalistic movement. Just looking at the incredible movement of a lizard or a bird, or even the smallest insect, can be a very humbling experience.*
—Jim Henson

At a friend's house in Maryland in the late 1940s, a young Jim Henson watched television for the very first time. He was hooked, and a genius was born. He simply *had* to find a way to get into TV—and in 1954, the summer after he graduated from high school, he did.

The *Junior Good Morning Show*, a local kid's program, was looking for puppeteers, and although he did not have any experience, he decided to try his hand at puppetry. He and a friend built a few puppets (his first were Pierre, the French rat, and two cowboy puppets, Longhorn and Shorthorn). They were hired, but the show only lasted a few weeks. Nevertheless, Henson had gotten his start.

While in college at the University of Maryland, Jim met Jane Nebel, his future partner and wife. Together they developed the Muppet style by working on several programs including *Sam and Friends*, a five-minute show that aired twice a day.

It was this program (it aired from 1955 to 1961) that first showcased Jim Henson's Muppets and allowed Henson to develop his craft. His first Muppet was actually born there, made from his mother's green spring coat and two halves of a Ping-Pong ball. Kermit was alive.

Although he was initially reluctant for his Muppets to join the cast of *Sesame Street* because he feared he'd be typecast as an entertainer just for children, Henson joined the team in 1969. With his work on *Sesame Street*, *The Muppet Show*, and his many other successful television and movie projects, Henson helped to make his Muppets popular cultural icons.

In 1990, Henson died of pneumonia. His sudden death was a shock to the world (including his extended *Sesame Street* and *Muppet Show* families). He is still greatly missed.

### ANIMATION CREATION

Few people know that Jim Henson was the creator of many of the "number animations" that ran during *Sesame Street*, the "Let's sing a song of two (or three, or four, etc.)" animations, and *"The King of 8."*

### THE OTHER SIDES OF HENSON

Jim's stranger creature creations and innovative effects have been seen in *The Dark Crystal*, *Labyrinth*, *The Storyteller*, *Dinosaurs*, *Fraggle Rock*, and in several other feature films and television productions like *The Muppet Show*.

*I find that it's very important for me to stop every now and then and get recharged and reinspired. The beauty of nature has always been one of the great inspirations in my life. I love to lie in an open field.*
—Jim Henson

Jim was incredibly kind. He judged you according to your ability
and always encouraged rather than criticized you. He never
raised his voice and he treated everyone the same, whether that
person was the janitor or the head of the network. He set a
wonderful example both as a human being and as a professional.
—Fran Brill

I will always remember Jim as the man who balanced
effortlessly between the sacred and the silly.
—Jerry Juel, writer

I think the one thing that impressed me almost more than anything else was that I don't think he ever spent a negative moment in his life.
—Bob McGrath

When I was young, my ambition was to be one of the people who made a difference in this world. My hope still is to leave the world a little bit better for my having been here.
—Jim Henson

The best thing of all was to watch Jim laugh until he cried…. I only now realize how important this man was that I worked and played with.
—Frank Oz

He loved directing and writing and producing, but most of all he
loved to perform with Frank and Jerry and all the puppeteers.
When we were little kids watching *Sesame Street*, we often felt
as if my father was performing just for us—but I think that he was
really just having a good time with his friends.
—Cheryl Henson

We miss his *spirit* even more than his creativity,
because he was also very good at training people, identifying
talented people, and giving them the space to grow.
—Loretta Long

# Frank Oz

### A MAN OF MANY VOICES

## Frank is as good as Lawrence Olivier when he's doing Grover.

—Arlene Sherman, supervising producer

**Movie Credits:** *The Muppet Movie, The Great Muppet Caper, The Muppets Take Manhattan, The Dark Crystal, The Empire Strikes Back,* and *The Return of the Jedi*
**Director of:** *In & Out, Dirty Rotten Scoundrels, Little Shop of Horrors, Housesitter, Indian in the Cupboard, The Muppets Take Manhattan*

You wouldn't think that the same man responsible for the straightlaced Bert is also responsible for the out-of-control Cookie Monster and the enthusiastically helpful Grover, but it's true. Frank Oz is a man of many voices.

## IN THE BEGINNING

Oz didn't always expect to be the man behind the furry blue monsters. In fact, he freely states that he had no

desire to be a puppeteer. "I just did it as a hobby to get some money—I really wanted to be a journalist," he says.

Oz was only seventeen years old when he met Jim Henson at a puppeteers' convention in California. They were friends and colleagues from then on. Oz started out as many Muppeteers do—as a right-hand man. His first job was as the right hand to a brown dog puppet named Rowlf on *The Jimmy Dean Show* (yes, the same Rowlf the Dog who later starred in *The Muppet Show*), one of Henson's first variety gigs. In the beginning, Oz says he wasn't confident enough to do voices. It took him about four years of performing before he felt comfortable speaking in character.

It's strange to think of that now, because all current Muppeteers agree that Oz is a *brilliant* manipulator and actor. He elevates everyone's performance with his ad-libs and his understanding of character and the curriculum. Oz, perhaps more than anyone else, can make us laugh hysterically one moment and tear up in the next. In the early years, Oz was in almost every skit. He now devotes four days a year to the show, and the producers and directors tape nearly fifteen new sketches with Bert, Grover, and Cookie on those days.

Jon Stone, former director, and Frank Oz with Supergrover

# Caroll

## THE MAN BEHIND THE BIRD

> One day I was looking at these Little Golden Books–I looked at the back and it said "Other titles you might enjoy," and there were Mickey Mouse and Minnie, Donald and Daisy Duck, Snow White, Dopey, Bambi, and Big Bird and Oscar. I've seen these wonderful characters all of my life, and now Big Bird and Oscar have joined the group!
>
> —Caroll Spinney on when he knew he'd made it

Spinney has been with *Sesame Street* ever since the first day when that big yellow bird ambled onto the street and that grouch popped up out of the can.

In 1969 in Salt Lake City, Spinney was approached by Henson after a somewhat disastrous performance at a puppet festival. It was only a few months before *Sesame Street* was about to go into production, and Henson was looking for a puppeteer to play "The Bird." "Everything went wrong with my big show," says Spinney of his program. "After the show, Jim came backstage and said to me, 'I liked what you were *trying* to do.'" A month later, Spinney was given the roles of Big Bird and Oscar the Grouch.

Initially, Spinney was told to play Big Bird as a somewhat goofy adult. But Spinney had a different feeling for the character. "I told the writers, 'I think he should just be a kid who is eight feet tall.'" So Spinney decided to use a higher pitched voice to make him younger. It worked—the character clicked, and thirty years later, he hasn't aged a bit.

"I'm still learning what to do with him," Spinney says. "The real secret of the Muppet's life is that the thought process is physically demonstrated.... If I put him at certain angles I can even get a smile out." Spinney loves being Big Bird—it's been his entire career. Big Bird has conducted the Boston Pops, met presidents, traveled to China—he's even been on the cover of *Time*. Not bad for a character who was originally referred to as just an eight-foot canary.

**Caroll Spinney has been a puppeteer since he was eight years old. By the time he was sixteen, his mother had made him more than seventy puppets. "My greatest satisfaction is that I'm doing exactly what I wanted to do as a child," he says today.**

## THE PERILS OF PUPPETRY

**Spinney's first Big Bird costume was extremely cumbersome, and it actually had to be buckled on, making it difficult to get in and out of quickly. This almost cost Spinney his life when a stage light crashed to the floor inches from where he was standing. Before anyone could stop it, the smoldering asbestos that came from the light caught the leg of Big Bird's costume on fire!**

**Thanks to a quick-thinking cameraman who clapped out the fire with his bare hands, Spinney escaped without serious injury. (No roasted chicken jokes, please.)**

**secret fact:**
Jim Martin (Oscar's right hand) usually plays Oscar when Big Bird and Oscar are required to be in a scene together. Spinney always does the voices for both puppets, however, and through the power of dual-channel stereo recording, no one ever notices.

> It's the same actor playing Big Bird and Oscar, which I'm sure has saved him thousands of dollars in therapy.
>
> —Sonia Manzano (Maria)

# Spinney

# Fran Brill

## FRAN AND ZOE

Fran Brill was the first female puppeteer to be hired on *Sesame Street*. She plays Zoe, the first main female Monster character. Brill is an extremely talented and funny puppeteer and actress who's also had a successful career away from the Street—a career that didn't require her to lie down on the ground and move a piece of cloth around with her hand.

Brill has done more theater than Prairie Dawn will ever do, on Broadway, off-Broadway, and nowhere even close to Broadway. She's been on soap operas, guest-starred on many television shows, including *Spenser for Hire* and *Law & Order*, and her movie credits include *Being There*, *What About Bob?*, and *Midnight Run*.

## THE LONG AND WINDING ROAD

Brill's Muppet career began in an agent's office during *Sesame Street*'s second season. She was in a Broadway play at the time and beginning to do voice-over and radio commercials. She was reading *Backstage*, a theatrical newspaper, when she came across an ad Jim Henson had run—he was looking for puppeteers for an upcoming Ed Sullivan Christmas special.

"He hired Richard Hunt and me—and that became the nucleus, with Frank, Jim, Jerry, and Caroll," Brill explains. "For me it was a kick. I had never even played with a puppet before. I laughed all the time. It was just a wonderful opportunity to hack around with a bunch of great guys."

## ERNIE'S RIGHT-HAND WOMAN

For a while, Brill did what most beginning Muppeteers did. She played supporting Anything Muppet roles, and was Ernie's right hand.

But even back then, she says, Prairie Dawn already existed—as an Anything Muppet. "She was just a docile, sweet little girl—never got her shoes dirty, she even carried a hanky back then. Now she's very liberated.

"I think Prairie was just a wonderful little character for Jim and Frank, because they played off her prissiness and her need to be Polly Perfect," Brill says. "Their objective became to make Prairie lose her cool and go ballistic. Cookie Monster was always looking under her skirt. We're all encouraged to be as idiotic as possible."

# JERRY NELSON

## YOU CAN COUNT ON HIM

Nelson is like the character actor you see one week on *Columbo*, the next on *The Love Boat*, and the next on *Murder, She Wrote*. You know and love his work, but he never gets the glory. That is, until now.

Nelson is one of the most versatile Muppeteers on the show. He can do gentle and gruff, nerdy and hip, human and monster, Martian and Twiddlebug, all with the greatest of ease. And he's been doing it ever since the show began.

## HOW NELSON GOT HIS START

Like most Henson Muppeteers, Nelson began working as a right-hand man (he replaced Frank Oz as Rowlf's right hand on the *The Jimmy Dean Show*). The Count, Mumford, and Herry are both two-handed puppets, and require the assistance of another Muppeteer.

Nelson's most famous and popular character is undoubtedly The Count, the vampire-esque Transylvanian who is obsessed with numbers. "People often say that I bear a strong resemblance to The Count. Now, I don't see it at all," Nelson says. The Count's purple, in the first place. But put Nelson in a cape and give him a monocle, and maybe, just maybe...

"The Count has always been fun just because he's so fixated with numbers," Nelson says. He thinks The Count loves numbers so much because "they're so pre-dictable." There's no doubt in his mind that if The Count didn't have his trust fund to keep him living in the cold damp castle of his dreams, he would have become a mathematician or a statistician.

## ALL HE EVER NEEDED TO KNOW HE LEARNED FROM *SESAME STREET*

Nelson has learned a lot of things from his Muppets over the years. Here are some of the more important lessons:

**Fat Blue (Grover's restaurant customer)**—Don't worry about poor service; learn to cook at home.

**Herry**—You can be strong and tender at the same time.

**The Amazing Mumford**—Don't give up, no matter how far away you are from the mark.

**The Count**—Take pleasure in the simple things. As many of them as possible.

# Kevin

## BEHIND EVERY TICKLISH MUPPET...

Kevin Clash does not look like a man who'd be playing a three-and-a-half-year-old Muppet with a high-pitched voice. More than six feet tall, with an athletic build, Clash looks like he'd be more at ease playing Herry or one of the larger monsters—not necessarily characters like Elmo and Baby Natasha.

When Clash began playing Elmo in 1984, he had no idea he'd make the character as popular as it's become. In fact, he wasn't that enthusiastic about playing Elmo at first. But that was just the beginning...

The character of Elmo had been played by two Muppeteers before Clash came along. Brian Meehl, who also originated Barkley and Telly, first played the little red Muppet, but left the show to pursue a writing career. Richard Hunt then took over the character, but admitted that he never found the character's true voice or motivation. Clash explains, "Richard's characters were very

loud, and very direct and very specific. The quiet Elmo wasn't a good fit with Richard's repertoire." Though Clash originally thought of Elmo as a hand-me-down, he made Elmo a much bigger personality than his diminutive size ever suggested.

Clash understood Elmo after he spent a summer watching his mother at work. "My mom is a day-care mother—she watches a lot of kids who are close to the age that Elmo is supposed to be. And I started thinking about that. The next season I came in, I had an idea what I was going to do."

That's when the character clicked. CTW finally started receiving letters and feedback that kids really liked the character, particularly Elmo's joyful and positive attitude. "Elmo always laughs, he just laughs about everything." But Clash remembers that the laugh initially bothered one of the show's directors, who set up a meeting with Clash to say, "You know, this laugh thing—it just doesn't work. I think you should do it less."

Little did the director know that a few years later, Tickle Me Elmo would make Elmo's trademark giggle the laugh heard 'round the world. In fact, Tickle Me Elmo was the number-one-selling toy in the world in 1996.

## IT'S BIGGER THAN US

Clash loves working on the show, and can't imagine doing anything else. The Tickle Me Elmo phenomenon—a feeding frenzy for the toy for Christmas 1996—proved to him how big the character had become and how loudly the show's message was being heard.

Despite all of the acclaim, Clash keeps his perspective clear: "The show is first and foremost about the kids, and you just don't get jaded when you keep that in your head." Clash explains that he also gained perspective from a letter Jim Henson wrote him in which Jim said, "Keep going. It's bigger than us."

# Clash

# Martin P. Robinson

**THE MAN BEHIND THE WORM
AND THE SNUFFLE**

> Marty Robinson's performance of Telly brings back memories of Bert Lahr doing the Cowardly Lion.... There is this really genuine angst and need which is somehow transformed into warmth.
>
> —Lou Berger, head writer for *Sesame Street*

Martin Robinson became a puppeteer so that he could play a wider variety of characters than his "nice guy" looks would have allowed him to play. "I wanted to do the weirdos, the strange things, the far-out things," says Robinson. "And who's gonna cast me in that—except as a puppeteer? So when I first started doing puppetry, all of a sudden there were no restrictions. You know, animals, vegetables, minerals, no gender requirements. I've played Slimey the Worm, who's three inches long, and Snuffleupagus, who's fifteen feet long."

Robinson's been with *Sesame Street* since 1979. He made his way there through various puppetry companies (including the famous Bil Baird's Marionettes, *the* puppet company to be in before Jim Henson reached popularity). He was also the designer and performer of the man-eating plant, Audrey II, in the original stage production of *Little Shop of Horrors*.

## WORKING THE STREET

Robinson's main characters are Snuffleupagus (the show's biggest character when it comes to sheer size) and Telly Monster (the show's biggest worrier). "Telly's a kid chronologically, but emotionally he's an old soul," Robinson says. "He's totally committed to whatever emotion he's feeling at any given time. When he's sad

he's just *devastated*, and when he's happy he's just *boundless*.... When he's worried about something he's just taken on the weight of the world. And he can switch gears on a dime, but that doesn't take anything away from how strongly he feels about any of those things."

He adds, "I'll never need heavy psychoanalysis as long as I have Telly."

Robinson also flexes his acting muscles as Slimey, the cute (but minute) companion of Oscar the Grouch. "The great thing about Slimey is that he *reveals* Oscar," Robinson says. "Oscar just adores Slimey. You can bring out all this wonderful heart of gold stuff."

Robinson is now one of *Sesame Street*'s senior Muppeteers, and even though the wear on his back might someday make getting into Snuffleupagus difficult, he fully expects to be working on the show for a long time to come.

"The wonderful thing about *Sesame Street* is that I spend most of my day laughing, having a good time, and hanging out with my friends. We're just havin' a ball here.... You'd expect a little bit of people saying, 'It's just a kid's show—it's not the cure for cancer.' But it brings light into the world as opposed to darkness. And it's a great thing to be a part of."

# Dear Sez Me: ANSWERING THE VIEWER MAIL

*Sesame Street* receives six to seven thousand letters each year, and responds to many of them. Here are a few that haven't been answered—until now. (Note: the letters are *real*—the responses are *not*.)

Dear Cookie Monster,
Who plays your voice on Sesame Street? Does he or she like cookies? I love cookies. Does he or she play another character on the show? On the show, when you eat cookies, are they real? How come your eyes never move? I know they are fake, but if they moved it would be better.
—AJ, Age 5

Dear AJ,
Me thank you for letter. It not only fun to read, it delicious! My voice performed by famous man named Frank Oz. Very talented. Big Hollywood director. Can afford to buy lotsa cookies. Frank like cookies very much, and yes, he performs many other characters on show—Grover and Bert, to name a couple. When I eat cookies, they are very real, and it *very important* that they stay that way, so no more letters like this or producers might think of clever way to save money. And me very sorry about my googly eyes. Cookie Mother told me not to cross them, but me not listen. They stuck. Do not try at home. Buh-bye.
—Cookie Monster

Dear Elmo,
Please, Elmo, come to our house and don't forget. You can bring Big Bird, too. When you come we will play and eat lunch. I will make macaroni and cheese and hot dogs. Elmo can have frut cottontail.
—Betsy, Age 4

Dear Betsy,
Elmo wants to play at Betsy's house, but Elmo can't drive yet. Also, Elmo is completely booked at the moment. Elmo will call you when his calendar is clear. Elmo and Betsy will do lunch.
—Elmo

Dear Sesame Street,
How old is Elmo? And tell Forgetful to write himself notes that will help him not to forget.
—Tiffany, Age 6

Dear Tiffany,
Elmo is three and a half years old. And Forgetful appreciates the tip—although for the life of him he can't remember what it was.
—Sez Me

Dear Sesame Street,
I was just wondering, was John Lennon ever on your show?
—Jenny, Age 16

Dear Jenny,
No, John wasn't. But the walrus was. Goo-goo-cachoo!
—Sez Me

Dear Sesame Street,

I need a piece of crucial information. I remember Ernie had a minature garden on his window sill. In this garden, he had what appeared to be milk cartons cut into the shape of little houses. My question is, what lived in these tiny homes and what were they called?
—Ben, Age 25

Dear Ben,

Here's your crucial information: The little characters are Twiddlebugs, tiny Muppet insects that use little everyday objects as their furniture. Try it for yourself someday. Get a big refrigerator box, make it into a house, and live on your neighbor's front lawn for a while. Fun, isn't it?
—Sez Me

Dear Oscar,
What do you do in your spare time?
—Manuel, Age 5

Dear Manuel,
Most of the time I sit alone in my can and think up mean things to say to people like you! Now scram!
—Oscar

Dear Sesame Street,
We used to watch Sesame Street when we were little and remember a character who played the piano. He would always make mistakes and would bang his head on the piano keys and say that he could never do it right. What is his name??
—Tanya, Tim, Katherine, and Dave, Ages 25–30

Dear Gang,
It was the extremely charismatic Mr. Barry Manilow.
Just kidding—it was Don Music.
—Sez Me

Dear Sesame Street,
I was wondering, who is older, Bert or Ernie?
—Jen, Age 4

Dear Jen,
Bert's older—you can see the wrinkles in his forehead.
Although that might just be stress.
—Sez Me

Dear Big Bird,
How 'bout this. You get me a present and I'll get you one, okay? I want one so badly. So if you by chance get me one, I'll write to you forever.
—Catelyn, Age 8

Dear Catelyn,
How 'bout this—you buy me the present first. Then we'll see how things go. 'Kay?
—Big Bird

Dear Sesame Street,
I hold a near and dear space in my heart for Sesame Street. It's a treasured part of my childhood mythology. I like to think that Cookie and I grew up together. We both eat better now. Sure, I know that zillions of people around the world have spent time on "my" street, but I still like to think of Sesame Street as my own secret place. Full of friends and adventure and a sense of communty that is precious. Thanks for keeping t safe for me.
—Sherrie, Age 29

Dear Sherrie,
We're always here for when you want to come home!
—Sez Me

"Hope you liked it.

NOW SCRAM!"

—Oscar the Grouch

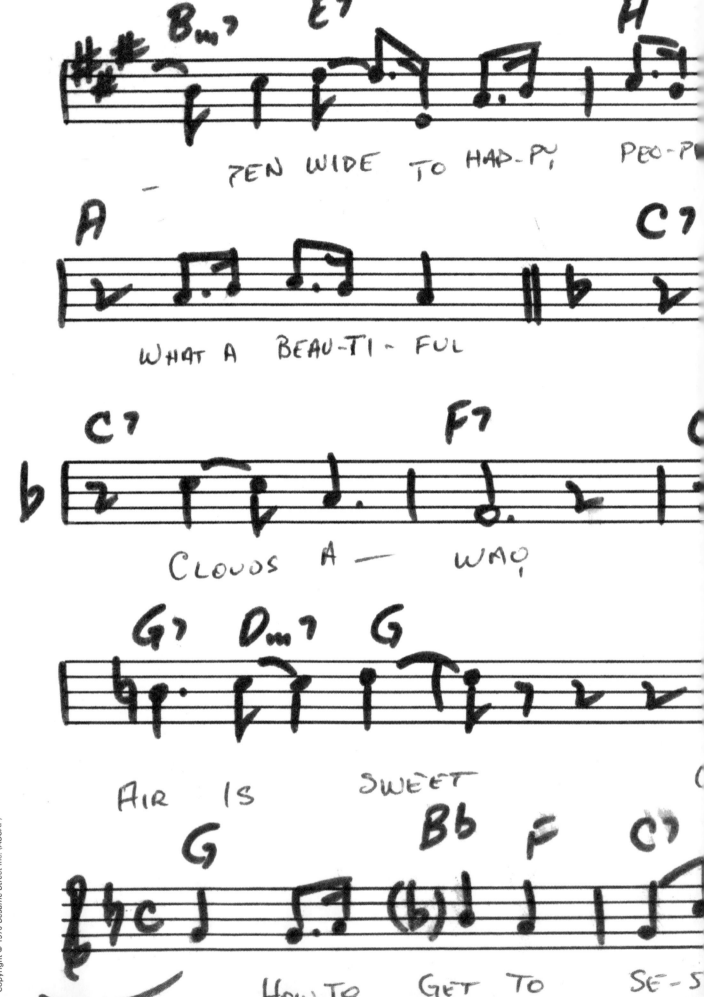